Roots and Trajectories of Violent Extremism and Terrorism

A Cooperative Program of
the U.S. National Academy of Sciences and
the Russian Academy of Sciences (1995-2020)

Glenn E. Schweitzer

Development, Security, and Cooperation

Policy and Global Affairs

The National Academies of
SCIENCES · ENGINEERING · MEDICINE

The views expressed are those of the author and
do not represent an official policy of the National Academies.

THE NATIONAL ACADEMIES PRESS
Washington, DC
www.nap.edu

THE NATIONAL ACADEMIES PRESS   500 Fifth Street, NW   Washington, DC 20001

This activity was supported by a contract with the Carnegie Foundation of New York. Any opinions, findings, conclusions, or recommendations expressed in this publication do not necessarily reflect the views of any organization or agency that provided support for the project.

International Standard Book Number-13: 978-0-309-08775-9
International Standard Book Number-10: 0-309-08775-9
Digital Object Identifier: https://doi.org/10.17226/26281

Additional copies of this publication are available from the National Academies Press, 500 Fifth Street, NW, Keck 360, Washington, DC 20001; (800) 624-6242 or (202) 334-3313; http://www.nap.edu.

Copyright 2022 by the National Academy of Sciences. All rights reserved.

Printed in the United States of America

Suggested citation: National Academies of Sciences, Engineering, and Medicine. 2022. *Roots and Trajectories of Violent Extremism and Terrorism: A Cooperative Program of the U.S. National Academy of Sciences and the Russian Academy of Sciences.* Washington, DC: The National Academies Press. https://doi.org/10.17226/26281.

The National Academies of
SCIENCES · ENGINEERING · MEDICINE

The **National Academy of Sciences** was established in 1863 by an Act of Congress, signed by President Lincoln, as a private, nongovernmental institution to advise the nation on issues related to science and technology. Members are elected by their peers for outstanding contributions to research. Dr. Marcia McNutt is president.

The **National Academy of Engineering** was established in 1964 under the charter of the National Academy of Sciences to bring the practices of engineering to advising the nation. Members are elected by their peers for extraordinary contributions to engineering. Dr. John L. Anderson is president.

The **National Academy of Medicine** (formerly the Institute of Medicine) was established in 1970 under the charter of the National Academy of Sciences to advise the nation on medical and health issues. Members are elected by their peers for distinguished contributions to medicine and health. Dr. Victor J. Dzau is president.

The three Academies work together as the **National Academies of Sciences, Engineering, and Medicine** to provide independent, objective analysis and advice to the nation and conduct other activities to solve complex problems and inform public policy decisions. The National Academies also encourage education and research, recognize outstanding contributions to knowledge, and increase public understanding in matters of science, engineering, and medicine.

Learn more about the National Academies of Sciences, Engineering, and Medicine at **www.nationalacademies.org**.

Contents

Introduction and Acknowledgments

During the past 25 years, the U.S. National Academies of Sciences, Engineering, and Medicine (the National Academies), in collaboration with the Russian Academy of Sciences (RAS), have carried out a wide variety of activities to improve understanding of the challenges in containing and reducing ethnic conflicts, violent extremism, and terrorism. More than 3,000 specialists from the two countries have been involved in these on-the-ground analytical and program activities. Initially, the focus was activities in Russia. More recently, mutual concerns have extended to disruptions and violence in other geographical regions as well. This report highlights challenges addressed by the academies over many years that remain of current interest as the U.S., Russian, and other governments continue to cope with old and new forms of aggression that threaten the livelihood of populations at home and abroad.

SCOPE OF THE REPORT

This report provides an overview of a cross-ocean program of U.S.-Russian nongovernmental cooperation that has focused on assessing the roots and trajectories of ethnic conflict, violent extremism, and terrorism during the past 25 years. The program has been based primarily on a series of bilateral agreements on scientific cooperation between the U.S. National Academy of Sciences (NAS) (which has been the lead U.S. organization) and the RAS, which in recent years has absorbed activities of the Russian Academies of Medical Sciences and Agriculture. Several activities have been sponsored primarily by other interested organizations in Russia. The overall program has involved American and Russian scientists, engineers, and medical professionals from a large number of government agencies, leading research institutions, think tanks, educational institutions, analytical centers, and consulting and commercial firms in the two countries.

In describing the cooperative activities that were carried out, the overview of the program set forth in this report underscores the importance of the many linkages between the nongovernmental activities of the NAS and the RAS and the directly related interests of the two governments. The program has included a broad range of analytical and exploratory activities that were designed to contribute to the following objectives:

- To improve understanding of the evolution and proliferation of violent extremism and terrorism, primarily in Russia, with increasing attention in recent years to terrorist threats in the United States and in other countries as well—in Central Asia, the Middle East, North Africa, and Europe.
- To highlight innovative steps by the U.S. and Russian governments for increasing the effectiveness of large programs in reducing threats of terrorism at home and abroad.
- To underscore approaches for curtailing the increasingly dangerous orientation and geographical spread of disruptive activities due to growing capabilities of some dissident groups.
- To suggest improved security approaches at the national, local, and institutional levels that could help prevent terrorists from disrupting stable conditions in many sensitive locations.

A particularly important development during the period of most active cooperation has been the continuing efforts of many disenfranchised groups to obtain and use increasingly potent technologies. Among the approaches of concern have been their capabilities to acquire dangerous radiological sources and materials, deadly biological agents, inexpensive but effective drones, and cyber technologies that can escalate the impacts of widely available weapons systems. In particular, several areas of the Middle East and Africa have increasingly become testing grounds for use of easy-to-deploy chemical weapons.

In contributing to international appreciation of many of the scientific dimensions of violence and terrorism, this report has been organized as follows:

- Limiting the development and spread of ethnic turmoil that has confronted a changing Russia (Chapter 1).
- Improving essential constraints on biological research and development activities (Chapter 2).
- Reducing vulnerabilities in protection of radiological sources during use, storage, and disposal (Chapter 3).
- Ensuring security of transportation, industrial, construction, and other activities involving dangerous materials, particularly in urban settings (Chapter 4).
- Addressing security challenges linked to recent ethnic turmoil in the Middle East and other areas of interest to the United States and Russia (Chapter 5).
- Increasing awareness of future political, economic, radiological, and other technological developments that could influence the direction of terrorism, and inter-academy plans to continue to move forward in improving understanding of the threats at various stages of violence (Chapter 6).

In addition, appendixes provide details of four important activities highlighted in the chapter narratives. Six other appendixes prepared by participants in recent engagement activities emphasize the relevance of discussions in different chapters to current and future developments in addressing ethnic relations, violent extremism, terrorism, and radiological challenges.

RELEVANT EXPERIENCE AND DOCUMENTATION

The period being considered was punctuated with changes in the U.S.-Russian political environment, which enabled an expansion of scientific interactions that began in the early 1990s. This new era of increased engagement permitted important sharing of security-related concerns between scientists, analysts, and current and future leaders in science, technology, and international relations.

Many of the activities of interest discussed have been documented in considerable detail in more than 30 analytical reports and proceedings of workshops published by the National Academies Press (NAP.edu). Also, the RAS and associated organizations have published or released a number of significant documents in Russian or English about inter-academy science cooperation during the period of interest. The most relevant and available documents have been identified in endnotes. In addition, many participants in the inter-academy activities have published other articles in various journals about their personal experiences and impressions during participation in the activities of the NAS and the RAS.

SCOPE OF THE JOINT ACTIVITIES OF THE NAS AND THE RAS

The activities that are highlighted represent greater than 70 percent of the program activities undertaken within the broader NAS-RAS program of exchanges in science-related activities during the past 25 years. The overall program of collaboration dates back to 1959. For more than 60 years, the program has addressed dozens of scientific and security issues confronting the two countries, including, but well beyond, terrorism-related challenges.

Devoting 70 percent of recent collaborative efforts to the science and security dimensions surrounding terrorism concerns has been a major commitment of financial resources and relevant expertise by the academies in both countries. The other 30 percent of inter-academy activities has been devoted to (a) joint endeavors of the Committees on International Security and Arms Control of the NAS and the RAS and (b) cooperative activities that have been oriented to other common interests involving the advancement and application of science. These other interests have included climate change, the energy-environment nexus, challenges for higher education at the graduate and postgraduate levels, commercialization of technology, genetically modified organisms, and developments in the Arctic region.

The cooperation during recent years that is considered has included (a) consultations between small groups of specialists from the two countries; (b) bilateral workshops, usually highlighted with prepared presentations by 20–30 specialists, followed by group discussions involving additional specialists; (c) on-site analyses of rapidly developing technologies by small groups of specialists from the two countries; (d) detailed studies of particularly challenging issues, which have been published; and (e) site visits by groups of 10 to 20 specialists.

Most events and related activities were carried out in Russia with visits to more than 30 facilities in Russia and about a dozen in the United States. These visits are identified in this report. A number of the most significant facilities were visited multiple times. Russian specialists had greater financial constraints on international travel than did their American counterparts. Therefore, fewer meetings and field visits were organized in the United States.

The organizers of the activities and the participants in the many wide-ranging meetings and related activities deserve credit for having provided the content of previous reports, which helped establish the framework for the overview set forth in this report.

Prior to 2012, many other organizations in the two countries, particularly governmental organizations, carried out much larger U.S.-Russian bilateral activities on terrorism than those implemented by the NAS and the RAS. Most of the intergovernmental efforts addressed events of immediate concern, and there was some overlap in the interests of the governments and the focus of the inter-academy program. In addition, a number of nongovernmental organizations beyond the academies in the two countries organized occasional U.S.-Russian meetings concerning developments related to terrorism. However, in more recent years, U.S.-Russian meetings focused on the science and technology dimensions of terrorism and related issues, other than those sponsored by the NAS and the RAS, have been limited in frequency and scope.

Finally, there have been several other characteristics of activities sponsored by the NAS and the RAS worth noting. (1) All American participants, other than the NAS staff, have been volunteers contributing their time for participation in the inter-academy program—with their only financial compensation being payment for travel and lodging. (2) The NAS-RAS programs were built on a base of 30 years of U.S.-Russian cooperation since the demise of the Soviet Union, with the RAS and other Russian participating organizations recognizing the NAS as an important partner during this period. At the same time, the RAS was also reliable in following through on commitments, while providing good conditions for inter-academy events in Russia. (3) As mentioned above, the NAS expended considerable effort in publishing peer-reviewed documents for almost all of the events that it sponsored, thereby maintaining its reputation as a reliable interlocutor for specialists with different points of view on topics of governmental interest, even during times of political uncertainties.

IMPORTANCE OF PEER REVIEW AND OTHER SUPPORT OF THIS REPORT

The peer reviewers of this report significantly improved the quality of the initial draft of the report. While the reviewers provided many constructive comments and suggestions, they were not asked to endorse the report's conclusions or recommendations nor did they see the final draft of the report. Thus, the responsibility for the final version of this report rests entirely with the author. The peer reviewers were as follows:

Cathy Ann Campbell, CRDF Global (retired);
Elena Filippova, Institute of Ethnology and Anthropology in Moscow;
Stepan Kalmykov, Lomonosov Moscow State University;
George Moore, Middlebury College;
Alexander Nechaev, Saint Petersburg Institute of Technology;
James Timbie, Stanford University.

Many American and Russian participants in the cooperative program obtained, organized, and presented the information that was consolidated in the many initial reports that provided the basis for this consolidated report. Also, NAS and RAS staff members served as the administrative backbone of the program, at home and abroad, and deserve special credit for sustaining an ambitious and productive array of activities during more than 25 years. Current staff members Amy Shifflette, Flannery Wasson, and Erik Saari made particularly important contributions to the preparation of this report.

FINANCIAL SPONSORS OF THE REPORT

The Carnegie Corporation of New York suggested the carrying out of this overview of past activities related to U.S.-Russian cooperation in addressing ethnic relations, extremism, and terrorism. Also, the corporation provided funding to support preparation of this report.

Many other U.S. organizations also provided support for the activities that are discussed in this report. In addition to the Carnegie Corporation, they included the Department of Defense, Defense Threat Reduction Agency; the Department of Energy (through the Brookhaven National Laboratory and the Pacific Northwest National Laboratory); the Department of State; the John D. and Catherine T. MacArthur Foundation; the Russell Family Foundation; the Richard Lounsbery Foundation; the Rutter Foundation; the Nuclear Threat Initiative; the Aleksanteri Institute of the University of Helsinki; and the National Research Council.

The details of Russian financial support for the program have not been available. Clearly, the Russian hosts provided important support and hospitality during events held in Russia, and Russian organizations covered a significant portion of the travel costs of their specialists abroad.

LEARNING FROM THE PAST TO INFORM THE FUTURE

Recognizing and understanding many of the dimensions of the threat of ethnic violence and terrorism activities at home and abroad will continue to be challenges for the scientific communities in both the United States and Russia. The opportunities for continued bilateral scientific cooperation are uncertain, but the lessons learned during 25 years of collaboration can provide a good basis for addressing problems of common interest that are likely to occur during the indefinite future.

ABOUT THE AUTHOR

Glenn E. Schweitzer has been the director of the Office for Central Europe and Eurasia of the National Research Council since 1985. From 1992 to 1994, he was on leave of absence to serve in Moscow as the chair of the Preparatory Committee for the Establishment of the International Science and Technology Center (ISTC) established by the governments of the United States, the European Union, Japan, and Russia. He then became the first executive director of the ISTC. Since 1989 he has written seven books and led the preparation of many reports on U.S.-Russian scientific cooperation, the proliferation of weapons of mass destruction, and high-impact terrorism.

1

Ethnic Conflicts within Russia

Better press coverage should be given to the life and activities of Chechens in Chechnya and outside its borders as part of the Russian community. Representation of them as noble savage people should be halted, showing instead how Chechens are building their lives and fighting against bandits. Special attention is warranted for coverage of entrepreneurial activities of the Chechens, which are both successful and useful for the country. Support for this sort of activities should also be provided by the authorities at various levels. Chechnya is a test of the new Russia's ability to correct its own tragic mistakes and respond to external threats. If we pass this test, peace will come to the Chechen Republic; and this means to all of Russia as well.[1]

– Perspective of 80 Russian and Chechen scholars and
policy officials at a conference in Moscow, 2000

The world at large has much to gain from better knowledge of causes, constraints, means of termination, methods of prevention, and processes of ethnic conflict settlement with regard to the violence in Chechnya and elsewhere. Superior knowledge of the situation would have a supremely practical advantage. It would improve the capacities of responsible specialists, officials, participants, and third parties to anticipate the consequences of alternative policies, and even to design creative non-violent ways of settling conflicts.[2]

– Global view of ethnic relations by
American Academician Charles Tilly, 2003

In some circumstances, ethnicity and religion are used in a competitive struggle for resources and power. The preservation of cultural diversity in a country's population and establishment of peaceful relations between different groups are complex but necessary for building a stable society. We need to have an adequate understanding of the role that ethnic and religious factors play in society and to develop and implement an effective state policy for maintaining cultural diversity.[3]

— Importance of ethnic and cultural diversity by
Russian Academician Valery Tishkov, 2005

OVERVIEW OF INTER-ACADEMY COOPERATION
IN ADDRESSING ETHNIC ISSUES

In February 2000, the Russian Academy of Sciences (RAS) unexpectedly proposed to the National Academy of Sciences (NAS) that the two academies undertake a joint program that addressed conflicts in multiethnic societies. The program would emphasize lessons learned in Chechnya and future approaches in reducing turmoil throughout the Caucasus region of Russia, while also addressing ethnic conflicts in other areas of the former Soviet Union. The NAS promptly agreed to join the RAS in bringing together well-qualified and influential scholars and practitioners in the two countries for carrying out this challenging endeavor.[4]

The ensuing program received high priority not only within the two academies but also within several U.S. foundations that provided financial support for collaborative NAS-RAS efforts to address ethnic conflict. Social scientists in both countries with extensive experience in addressing ethnic unrest in various areas of the world participated in a series of interrelated activities over a period of more than 7 years. Scientists who had moved to Moscow from Grozny in Chechnya in the wake of increasing violence in the Caucasus were also asked to play key roles in the analyses and search for approaches to reducing ethnic hostilities. Box 1-1 identifies the many inter-academy activities that were carried out.

At the outset of collaboration in addressing ethnic challenges, the NAS team quickly recognized that a group of researchers at the Institute of Ethnology and Anthropology in Moscow was among the best informed and most influential scientists focusing on turmoil in Chechnya. Also, the Institute of Sociology had a strong team of researchers devoted to ethnic problems in Russia. It was clear to all that this topic had become a core security issue

BOX 1-1
Chronology of Events Concerning
Multiethnic Challenges

February 2000: RAS proposes a project on conflicts in multiethnic societies.

April–June 2000: NAS team visits Moscow, agreement is reached on the goals for a project, and the new project begins.

October 2000: NAS team meets in Moscow with Russian officials and scholars and then travels to Rostov-on-Don for further consultations with specialists from five republics in the Caucasus region.

December 2000: RAS hosts a symposium in Moscow attended by 80 Russian and Chechen scholars and 10 American and European specialists.

June 2001: Valery Tishkov and other Russian specialists travel to Washington, D.C., for consultations with American scholars and for planning of the next phase of the project.

September–October 2001: NAS representatives visit Moscow to discuss the overall program and Kazan, where the focus is on education. Three NAS-RAS working groups are formed, and they begin corresponding electronically.

November 2001: In Nizhny Novgorod, a roundtable of managers of an early warning network to assess ethnic unrest provides important insights for the NAS team, and discussions are held with government officials of the Volga Federal District. As a follow-up, Sergey Kirienko, representative for the Volga Federal District and subsequently prime minister of Russia, delivers a lecture at the NAS in Washington, D.C., in 2002.

December 2001: NAS-RAS working groups meet in Washington, D.C., to discuss research priorities and to meet with policy officials. A capstone workshop is held to begin preparation of a key report. During the workshop, President Putin sends a message to Washington to inform Professor Vladimir Zorin that he has been appointed minister for nationalities and is needed immediately in Moscow.

April 2002: NAS-RAS team visits Kazan with a focus on education and on disputes with the Russian government over the economic benefits from extraction of oil resources "belonging" to the region.

continued

BOX 1-1 Continued

September 2002: NAS, RAS, Chechen, and European experts meet in Sochi to discuss education challenges. Also, agreement is reached on a 12-month program of outreach activities in Chechnya with a focus on opportunities for the youth.

September 2003: Workshop in Moscow focuses on approaches by district-level governments in combating ethnic-oriented terrorism, particularly in Dagestan.

2004: NAS, in collaboration with RAS, requests funding from the NATO-Russia Council for support of significantly expanded efforts concerning interethnic challenges to include European, French, and U.K. experts. After 1 year of positive deliberations, the NATO-Russia Council turns down the proposal.

2006: Report of an NAS-RAS–sponsored workshop in Finland on roots and routes of democracy and extremism is published.

2007–2017: NAS and RAS retain interest in collaboration within the context of counterterrorism, as discussed in Chapter 4. In 2017, ethnically based violent extremism again becomes an important component of inter-academy activities, as discussed in Chapter 5.

---

as the new Russia adjusted to deep-rooted political challenges at home and abroad. As to available analyses of the chaos in Chechnya and other turbulent areas, the Kona Statement that was prepared in 1994 at a retreat in Hawaii by a group of leading American, Russian, and East European ethnologists had become a particularly important document in academic circles in Moscow when addressing ethnic relations within Russia (see Appendix A).

As noted in Box 1-1 and discussed throughout this chapter, this new inter-academy cooperative program involved a variety of activities. In addition to reviews of published papers on dealing with ethnic relations in many areas of the world, the participants ploughed new ground. Joint analyses of specific troublesome issues by small teams of Russian and American scientists were undertaken. They prepared individually authored papers and institutional publications based on meetings and workshops in Moscow, Rostov-on-Don, and Sochi within the framework of the new effort. Consultative visits by Russian and American scientists to several municipalities in the North Caucasus, to Kazan, and to Nizhny Novgorod provided access to local perspectives. A few small innovative field projects centered in Chechnya helped transform theory into practice. A multifaceted workshop in Washington, D.C., brought together perspectives of core concerns. Finally, an international workshop in Helsinki offered fresh perspectives of experts from Europe and the Middle East as well as researchers from the United States and Russia whose experiences challenged and then supported the views of core members of the overall program team.

For several additional years, the two academies continued their collaboration in developing frameworks for follow-on activities. However, additional NAS-RAS activities within these frameworks were not carried out due to changes in priorities of potential financial sponsors. A particular disappointment was the loss of interest of the NATO-Russia Council in providing financial support for an ambitious extension of the program to address increasingly difficult ethnic challenges throughout Europe. This initiative was supported by the U.K., French, and Russian governments. However, at the staff level of the council, the proposal seemed too complicated to implement under the sponsorship of NATO, since many members of the council consistently questioned the intentions of Russian organizations.

SIGNIFICANT ANALYSES AND FINDINGS

At a capstone workshop in Washington, D.C., in 2003, NAS and RAS specialists reported their findings on developments in Chechnya and several other "hot spots" in Russia. The conclusions were based in large measure on the early activities identified in Box 1-1. In a report that was strongly supported by well-known ethnologists and political scientists from the two countries, the findings called for 10 research themes to be given priority by government funding organizations in Washington and Moscow that were interested in such analytical efforts.[5] At the same time, other nongovernmental institutions that supported social science researchers and analysts in fields of broad international interest were invited to join the effort. The themes were as follows:

1. Studies of social processes with examination of how groups and conflicts are defined and how participants align themselves along religious, political, racial, and regional lines.
2. Investigations of social processes that move ethnic conflict into or out of violent forms of struggle.

3. Analyses of how political entrepreneurs, violence specialists, and dealers in contraband promote and inhibit transitions between violent and nonviolent forms of struggle.

4. Studies of how combinations of different forms of governmental authority and population compositions promote or inhibit acute conflicts associated with ethnic groups.

5. Compilations of extensive and comparable catalogs of conflict events before, during, and after the collapse of the Soviet Union.

6. Detailed investigations of the effectiveness of interventions in ethnic conflicts.

7. Carrying out of complementary comparative studies of social changes in localities and regions to identify precipitants of serious conflicts and to look closely at the inhibition, mitigation, and termination of conflicts.

8. Analyses of varying state policies for protection, recognition, representation, and repression of ethnic minorities.

9. Impact of legal systems on the extent and character of ethnic conflict.

10. Effects of changes in the forms of communications—such as the impact of changes in access to television and to the internet—on ethnic mobilization, conflict, violence, and conflict resolution.[6]

Associated with the centrality of this list of priorities were insightful observations of developments in Chechnya by Valery Tishkov, the director of the Institute of Ethnology and Anthropology. For example, he underscored the following challenges:

Words can be very important components of violence. Armed conflict in Chechnya started with the legitimization through verbal expression and introduction of such slogans as national revolution and national self-determination as well as statements about nation-killing and Russian imperial domination. Some works by Chechen authors, numerous publications by Russian historians, and nationalist brochures from other parts of the former Soviet Union portraying a heroic Chechen history and calling for correction of past injustices contributed to the outbreak of violence. Scientific conferences involving prominent leaders of the liberation movement aired not only mythical versions of the past but direct appeals to complete the mission of liberation.

It is important to determine the point wherein all these words are transformed into bullets, although the link between verbal insults and direct violence is often rather peculiar. As a rule, those who put forward ethnic-related appeals or develop moral or ideological justifications rarely join in the fight themselves. Fighters are recruited from different groups. Most often they are recruited from among young men in rural areas or on urban margins. That is the situation with numerous jihads, liberation attacks, revolutions, and other collectively violent movements. Different players, often changing the very nature of these appeals, will relay academic and other calls to action. With the escalation in violence, initial slogans are not only transformed beyond recognition, they quite often are simply forgotten.[7]

VIEWS FROM THE REPUBLICS AND BEYOND

At the outset of the project, an inter-academy workshop in Rostov-on-Don attracted researchers from eight republics located in the Caucasus region. They made more than a dozen well-prepared presentations on ethnic rumblings in their regions and their difficulties in accepting the increasing number of edicts on conciliation published in Moscow. It seemed clear from remarks by the workshop participants that *nationalism* was replacing *religious commitments* as the basis for complaints from the region. Almost all participants bemoaned problems in adjusting to the politically charged economic policies and practices within their boundaries. Some objected to Kremlin-decreed changes in governance practices, while others reported favorably on many governmental modifications and clarifications in addressing ethnic-related complaints that they considered long overdue.[8]

Regional officials, in a separate meeting with the NAS and the RAS specialists, persuasively argued that their efforts to promote equality throughout the region were constantly undermined by policies emanating from Moscow. While the central government in principle promoted economic development from farming to generation of nuclear power, there were limits on the initiatives that could be influenced by local perspectives. A particularly sensitive issue was the personal interests of members of the leadership in the republics and the compilation of excessive wealth by local organizations or individuals who were not moving forward in lockstep with the policies of the federal government.[9]

At that time, an important issue that began to resonate throughout Russia and remained a frontline issue for many years concerned the process for selecting the governor for each region—either appointment by the Kremlin or, alternatively, selection by the local population. The policy was changed several times, and only in 2016 did the Kremlin stop the switching of its position and decreed that decisions on appointments of governors would be made in Moscow. The one exception that then became and remained the law for the indefinite future proclaims that the governor of Chechnya will continue to be locally elected and will control all security forces, including the 30,000 military and KGB personnel, who had been stationed in the republic for many years.[10]

Later, during the explorations in various regions, American scientists visited Nizhny Novgorod to discuss the ethnoreligious accord adopted in the Volga Federal District. This accord provided an important window for understanding the diversity of ethnic conflicts and approaches to reducing conflicts in Russia. The widely publicized program of the district identified many challenges in reducing animosities.

Another venue for exploring interfaith challenges in Russia was in the city of Kazan, with a population of 1.2 million people. This capital of the Republic of Tatarstan is located in the heartland of Russia. When the specialists from the two academies visited, local animosity toward Kremlin policies was continuing to reflect the growing importance of ethnic groups. There were three particularly divisive challenges. Fortunately, practical solutions toward conciliation were underway in each of the areas set forth below:[11]

- On the economic front, the leadership of the Tatars bitterly contested the policies emanating from Moscow that gave the Russian government control over all of the income from extraction of the oil resources within Tatarstan. Republic officials considered that the oil belonged to Tatarstan—not to Russia. As interethnic violence continued to erupt on many fronts over the economic health throughout the republic, the Kremlin agreed to allow the republic to have a carefully negotiated percentage of revenues associated with the extraction and sale of oil on Tatarstan territory. This action went a long way to bringing internal calm throughout the Tatar community.
- A second issue was the dispute over the language to be used in secondary schools—Russian or Tatar or even English as the primary language. During the visit to Kazan by members of the NAS

team involved in the inter-academy program, it appeared that the language issue had been resolved, at least in the most prosperous areas of the city. A visit to one of the premier high schools confirmed that classes in this school were being offered in one or more of the three languages, with the families of the students permitted to choose the languages that they preferred. At the school—and reportedly at other selected schools—students were able to take a few courses in English, particularly in science for which there were available textbooks in English. Other courses such as history and social sciences were usually conducted in either Russian or Tatar. This system seemed to be working well, as many of the students became trilingual.

- Regarding the language issue at the university level, where Russians filled many of the professorial posts, there was considerable resistance to allowing courses to be offered in the Tatar language. At Kazan State University, the situation did not seem complicated, with professors arguing that it was ridiculous to teach science courses in Tatar when all of the books were in Russian or English. Still other professors were trying to accommodate the advocates of teaching in Tatar to the extent possible, arguing that job competitions often called for fluency in the Tatar language.

Another area of concern was Dagestan, and particularly the region along the coast of the Caspian Sea. Terrorism was becoming a common practice of the opposition in confronting the local government that had made deals with their neighboring countries for the transportation of oil resources from the Caspian Sea. A symposium on this issue was organized in Moscow by the RAS, at a time when explosions disrupting pipelines were common occurrences. The project involved specialists from the United States, Russia, and Dagestan. The RAS published a much-needed book documenting activities in Dagestan, drawing heavily on the symposium.[12]

Near the end of this phase of the inter-academy program, the NAS and the RAS organized a workshop in Finland to obtain broader international insights into violent extremism that was resulting in loud alarms throughout the Middle East and Europe. Some participants were particularly interested in the recruitment incentives used by ISIS and other radical groups in the search for foreign fighters from Chechnya and Europe. Three Russian participants made important comments that clarified arguments they set forth at home. These comments included the following observations:

- A Russian specialist on developments in the Caucasus and Central Asia pointed out that the extremism of the North Caucasus Wahhabists was an enormous problem that could not be resolved by force. Neither could it simply be settled through discussions, since the ideology itself does not allow for any negotiation with atheists. In the dangerous view of this sect, a state built on "human" laws should be destroyed. Only divine laws should prevail in the world. At the same time, some Muslim radicals considered Western democratic tendencies a good idea, giving them an opportunity for an honest struggle to convince the populations of the righteousness of their vision of further social development. Of course, extremists consider democracy to be an evil human invention, fundamentally harmful inasmuch as it does not conform to clear divine regulation of the social order. He urged removal of the social basis for the extremists through economic development, increased living standards for the population, and establishment of normal dialogs involving the region's Muslim community.[13]

- Next were the following comments from a Russian expert on the Middle East and North Africa. Despite obvious failures in economic, technological, and material development throughout the Muslim world, there had been a powerful expansion of Islam—from South Africa to the banks of the Volga, the Rhine, and the Thames and across the United States. How does Islam attract new converts? Maybe by a lack of hierarchism and widespread egalitarianism, which lends dignity and respect to the followers of the religion. Perhaps by its hospitality, which is more widespread among Muslims than in most societies. Is the attraction its institutionalized charity system, which supports the poor? Like other religions, Islam advocates unachievable ideals. But the goals exist. By quoting phrases out of context from the Koran, as well as from the Gospels and the Bible, one can explain anything.[14]

- The third commentator had unfettered access to closely protected Russian literature on extremism. He asserted that a major part of the political elite recognized the corruption and inefficiency of law enforcement agencies. Reforms should not be limited to firing employees who apply their own extremist views in their daily work. Reforms should be introduced in a manner that at least changes the atmosphere, if not the ideology, within law enforcement agencies, and in particular the attitudes toward migrants. With regard to education, he concluded that the younger generation receives no humanist education, while young teachers are particularly receptive to leftist ideology. There are alternatives to the approaches of capitalist societies, including humanist ideas in education programs as an important strategic task.[15]

MONITORING OF ETHNIC RELATIONS

Also of considerable interest was the design and implementation of a national ethnic monitoring network that operated in many regions of Russia and in several areas of neighboring countries beginning in 1994. The network, which is described in Appendix B, galvanized interest of local officials and researchers throughout many regions of the country to improve understanding of the roots of ethnic anxieties that could lead to violence. The Institute of Ethnology and Anthropology has coordinated the network that monitors ethnic relations across Russia and in other parts of the former Soviet Union. Signals of ethnic unrest have been used by local hosts who maintain the network as a basis for actions to prevent escalation of tensions. The actions have taken a variety of forms ranging from simple conciliatory discussions with aggrieved parties, to informal agreements resolving inappropriate actions, to pressure from local authorities to adopt more reasonable demands that could be settled informally or legally.

The results of dispute resolutions have been shared in general terms at scientific seminars with members of the network to evaluate the sociopolitical situations in their states or regions based on 46 indicators of potential turbulence in the following categories:

- Environment and Resources
- Demography and Migration
- Power, State, and Politics
- Economics and the Social Sphere
- Culture Education and Information
- Contacts and Stereotypes
- External Conditions

The findings of current surveys have been compiled and compared with data from previous years to determine the changing level of ethnic tensions in specific geographical areas over time. From its earliest days, this approach was repeatedly cited by specialists throughout Russia and neighboring countries as a success story, since indicators that were shining red could attract attention of local authorities or interested nongovernmental parties such as the church to take early action and prevent escalation of disputes. The network compiled hundreds of examples of how early actions to resolve relatively minor disputes quelled hostilities before they erupted into difficult confrontations. This monitoring approach was adopted but modified by a few specialists facing similar challenges in other countries as they sought the levers to suppress the drivers of terrorism and to emphasize steps that could lead to harmony and understanding.

The world has changed in dramatic ways since back-of-the-envelope calculations were initially used in weighing evidence of ethnic harmony or disruption that was reported. But few will dispute the importance of continuous monitoring of ethnic-related aspirations in areas in turmoil. When such monitoring leads to efforts to predict and prevent conflict, support becomes widespread.

A MODEST PROJECT DIMENSION OF THE QUEST FOR CALM IN CHECHNYA

When the NAS was invited to join with the RAS in seeking roads to a reduction in violence, initially focused on Chechnya, there was no shortage of Russian and international academics who were prepared to write papers and present theories about steps to settle the rumblings among the population of Chechnya. But simply writing academic papers, however persuasive, and then organizing workshops to provide the basis for more papers were viewed by many as an inadequate response to the call from the RAS to join forces with the NAS in addressing on-the-ground realities in Grozny. On-the-ground activities to start the process of turning the society away from violence and onto the road for improved understanding and peace were desperately needed.

As a token start, the NAS committed $20,000 of internal funds to seed a few projects in Chechnya that offered hopes that life could improve in the wayward republic where nationalism had begun to replace religion as the basis for complaints.[16] In retrospect, the limited amount of funds that became available, even with several modest supplements, was shockingly low. But at the time, the economic situation for the general population was very desperate, as many families were seeking money at any level by any means for survival.

The RAS and the NAS decided to focus the small collaborative program activities on the youth and on education. In September 2002, the academies convened a workshop in Sochi, which was attended by 10 educational leaders in Chechnya. They and 15 other participants from Russia, Europe, the United States, and Chechnya were well prepared to discuss the challenges of education, to review a new report by the United Nations Educational, Scientific and Cultural Organization (UNESCO) for revitalizing higher education in Chechnya, and as always to discuss the future of Chechnya more broadly. At the same time, the Chechen educators presented 15 proposals for small pilot projects in the battered territory.

The discussion of the draft of the UNESCO report was lively. While education officials in Moscow were well intended in working with UNESCO to prepare a report that recognized many of the unique aspects of changing approaches in Grozny, local educators from Chechnya were only marginally involved in the report preparation. Nevertheless, they welcomed new attention on the desperate situation.[17]

The report offered a vision of modern approaches to education, even in a war-torn republic. However, the difficulty in traveling on the proscribed path to realize the education goals was based in large measure on fantasy—a fantasy of availability of transportation to and from school, a fantasy that willing and able local teachers would always be available, a fantasy that education in Grozny would put them on the road to professional success, and a fantasy that children could be spared from the horrors of internal warfare.

However, within 3 days of workshop discussions the local educators had succeeded in adding a broad dose of reality to the road ahead. They were satisfied in their amendments to the draft of the UNESCO report. Highlighting the need for revision of the report was one of the most promising contributions on the road to reconstruction that the NAS and the RAS made during their 6 years of cooperation focused on Chechnya and surrounding environments.

Mini-Projects Focused on the Youth of Chechnya

Turning to the proposals for mini-projects, six were initially selected for support.[18] They were as follows:

1. Establishing a museum of local folklore for hosting regional folk festivals at Grozny Middle School No. 58. As this story began to emerge, teenage students cleared remains from the crumbling walls of a bombed-out building; and then several thousand dollars provided by the NAS were used to buy material for floors, walls, and ceilings of three rooms where artifacts reflecting the history of Chechens and the territory of Chechnya were to be on display. The artifacts contributed by local residents reflected lifestyles of the Chechen population over many decades. They included modest clothing, celebratory costumes and caps, hand tools and farm implements, and cookware and dining facilities, for example.

2. Using distance learning in mathematics to improve the skills of pre-university students who lived in the highlands 10 and more miles distant from Grozny. However, the concept of independent learning combined with occasional interactions with teachers was not well understood. In short order, the absence of good communications and lack of adequate written material led to abandonment of this project.

3. Organizing a student essay contest on approaches toward settling the conflict in Chechnya and priorities for reconstruction. Law students at Chechen State University prepared 10 original essays that were translated into English and distributed locally and internationally. While the essays contained interesting ideas, the appropriate officials for considering the suggestions were stretched so thin that they had little interest in giving credence to the views of "inadequately informed" students. Among the topics that were addressed were the following:
   - Organizing Programs on Democratization of Society
   - Ensuring the Security, Rights, and Freedom of Citizens
   - Shaping International Public Opinion on the Situation in Chechnya
   - Considering Captured Members of the Resistance not as Criminals but as Persons Seeking a Return to Peace
   - Guaranteeing Personal Security for Recipients of Amnesty

- Discontinuing Arrests of Local Residents Who Looked like Chechens
- Recognizing Illegality of the Exile of Chechens en masse to Central Asia
4. Preparing textbooks on Chechen literature for grades 10 and 11. Prominent scholars in Moscow and Grozny prepared books, with scripts too often based on their partisan views on the situation in Chechnya and with inadequate concern over different views on approaches to education.
5. Establishing a job placement center at Chechen State University. Unfortunately, all available jobs were in locations where it was too dangerous to live.
6. Equipping a sports hall for freestyle wrestling competitions linked to the physical education curriculum of Grozny Teachers College. According to Russian visitors who photographed activities at the college, this initiative was a resounding success. The limited NAS funds were used to buy mats and other equipment for wrestling matches for young men that provided an after school alternative to their roaming of the streets armed with Kalashnikov rifles.

THE IMPORTANCE OF ETHNO-RELIGIOUS DIALOGUES

In closing this chapter, it is instructive to cite the following axioms that highlighted the comments of forward-looking realists in Nizhny Novgorod. Individuals may be tolerant toward friends or persons close to them who are of a different faith or nationality, but they may be xenophobes and racists in a broader social environment (at work, in politics, or in creative work).

- Relying on dialogues and consensus is more difficult than engaging in rejection and hostility, for the latter requires no special efforts on personal development when it is connected with a limited outlook and ignorance.
- The most diverse forms of intolerance may exist and be manifested in democratic societies, and the task of the state and society is to prevent their extreme (including violent) forms, which threaten the foundations of social order and statehood.
- It is necessary to combat opponents of peace and supporters of violence not only with public condemnation campaigns but also with other effective methods such as public rejection, judicial

prosecution, education, and even their inclusion in the systems of institutions of power and civil society.

- Efforts to establish ethno-religious harmony and prevent conflicts demand sacrifice and the best human qualities, but they may produce results only if carried out jointly and with the support of the state.

- Strong government and prosperous living conditions do not guarantee peace and harmony, and conflicts among representatives of the elite are more frequent and stronger than those among the common people. However, order and prosperity provide increased opportunities to avoid intolerance, violence, and conflicts.[19]

Additional comments on cooperation about ethnic challenges during later years are set forth in Chapter 5 and Appendix E.

NOTES

1. NRC (National Research Council). 2003. *Conflict and Reconstruction in Multiethnic Societies: Proceedings of a Russian-American Workshop*. Washington, DC: The National Academies Press, p. 194.
2. Ibid., Tilly, C., "Priorities for Research on Conflict in Multiethnic Communities," p. 2.
3. Tishkov, V. 2004. *Network for Ethnic Monitoring and Early Warning*. Moscow: Institute of Ethnology and Anthropology, Russian Academy of Sciences, p. 3.
4. Op. cit., NRC, p. viii.
5. Ibid., p. 1–5.
6. Ibid.
7. Ibid., p. 38.
8. Ibid., p. 195–196 and staff notes during visit to Rostov-on-Don.
9. Ibid.
10. Ibid., observations supported by Professor Sufian Zhemukho, George Washington University (expert on developments in Caucasus), February 21, 2020.
11. Ibid., p. 201–208 and staff notes during visit to Kazan.
12. Institute of Ethnology and Anthropology. 2003. *Symposium on International Views on Developments in Dagestan*. Moscow: Russian Academy of Sciences.
13. Yarlykapov, A. A. 2006. "Radicalism and Extremism of Muslim Populations of the North Caucasus: Ideology and Practice," in *Proceedings of a Workshop: Roots and Routes of Democracy and Extremism*, T. Hellenberg and K. Robbins, eds. Helsinki: Aleksanteri Institute, University of Helsinki, p. 183.
14. Ibid., Vassiliev, A., "Islamic Extremism as a Manifestation of the Crisis of Muslim Civilizations," p. 46.
15. Ibid., Mitrokhim, N., "Non-Islamic Extremism in Contemporary Russia," p. 168.
16. Schweitzer, G. E. 2004. *Scientists, Engineers, and Track-Two Diplomacy*. Washington, DC: The National Academies Press, p. 76.

17. Ibid.
18. Ibid.
19. Op. cit., NRC, "Program for Strengthening Ethno-Religious Accord in the Volga Federal District," p. 201.

Student Folklore Museum established in Chechnya in 2002 with financial support by the NAS.
Source: Photograph provided by the NAS.

2

Acceptable Limits on Biological Research

Reproducing intensively and colonizing territories, humankind itself creates new possibilities for the reproduction, spread, and variation of infectious pathogens. Nature is the world's chief bioterrorist. Increasing our joint potential for control of emerging and yet unpreventable infections will provide us with more options for preventing any kind of bioterrorism, be it deliberate or generated by nature.

> – Sergey Netesov, Russian leader of NAS-RAS studies and workshops on countering bioterrorism, 2007[1]

When the anthrax fermenter is relegated to the scrap heap and its operator is retired, how do we increase the likelihood that the next generation of molecular biologists and virologists, with much better tools and knowledge, will continue to work for the "good" of their people, their country, and the global community? This is an opportunity for partnerships in the life sciences.

> – David Franz, U.S. leader of NAS-RAS studies and workshops on countering bioterrorism, 2014[2]

We believe in the essential need for Russian-American cooperation in the following areas:

- *Epidemiology, virology, and molecular biology studies of COVID-19 and its variants, origins, genetics, and mutations.*

- *Pathophysiological aspects of the coronavirus, methods of diagnostics, treatment, and prevention of this disease and its spread.*
- *Mathematical modeling and computer modeling of the global pandemic and its spread around the world.*
- *Social economics and psychological effects of the pandemic and methods of assessing, mitigating, and overcoming its negative effects and interconnected emerging humanitarian risks and needs.*
- *Strengthening global security from biological threats.*
  – Joint Protocol on Cooperation Concerning COVID-19, Signed by the presidents of the Russian Academy of Sciences, National Academy of Sciences, National Academy of Engineering, and National Academy of Medicine, September 2020

BIOLOGICAL RESEARCH BECOMES AN INTER-ACADEMY PRIORITY

For four decades, the Committees on International Security and Arms Control (CISAC) of the National Academy of Sciences (NAS) and the Russian Academy of Sciences (RAS) have been interested in the dangers of bioterrorism. During the early 1980s, reports began to emerge about the 1979 contamination of the soil with anthrax near a military facility in Sverdlovsk (now Yekaterinburg) far to the east of Moscow. While Soviet scientists claimed that the contamination resulted from the natural presence of anthrax in farmlands where cattle grazed and then spread the anthrax to the population, there were suspicions that the anthrax was accidently emitted from the military facility that was illegally producing anthrax in a form that could be used for military purposes in violation of the Biological Weapons Convention (BWC). This controversy was discussed at length by U.S. and Russian experts under the umbrella of the parallel CISAC committees. Eventually, violation of the BWC was documented.

Then in the 1990s, as the integrity of the BWC remained of concern, the two academies decided to put a long-term spotlight on cooperation in addressing biological research with potential dual-use implications. While the CISACs remained concerned about violations of the BWC, the new programs that were undertaken and that are the theme of this chapter extended beyond the responsibilities of the parallel CISAC committees.

Programs were initially supported by the Department of Defense, Defense Threat Reduction Agency (DOD/DTRA). Increasingly, other

U.S. government departments and private foundations learned about the inter-academy program's influence in facilitating contacts and assessing positive impacts of collaborative efforts in addressing biological challenges. They also turned to the NAS for assistance in mounting programs in Russia.

In 2002, 5 years into the NAS-RAS program, the spread of anthrax-laden letters in the United States and the threat of such letters being sent within Russia heightened concerns about the capabilities of both countries to adequately control dangerous biological agents. These concerns were amplified by questions over the purposes of the Iranian recruitment of Russian bioscientists for employment in Tehran. Also, anxieties about the expanded dimensions of bioterrorism were raised when criminals attempted to contaminate a Moscow marketplace with infected chickens to shift customers to a competitive market nearby.[3] Box 2-1 sets forth the chronology of particularly significant cooperative activities over two decades that involved the NAS in various ways.

Most of these activities were also supported by the RAS, with a few dependent on direct cooperation with other Russian organizations.

BOX 2-1
Milestones in NAS Cooperation with Russian Partners

1995: Direct contact of the NAS with Biopreparat leadership and a follow-up U.S.-Russian workshop near Moscow.

1996: International conference in Kirov.

1997: U.S. and Russian experts agreed that a major initiative concerning dangerous pathogens was imperative.

1997–1998: Eight pilot bioresearch projects developed by the NAS carried out at two key Russian research institutes.

1998–2009: Long-term commitment of the DOD/DTRA to support NAS biocooperation with Russian partners.

1998–2000: In response to a request from the DOD/DTRA, reviews by the NAS of 80 bioresearch proposals that had been submitted by Russian scientists to the DOD/DTRA.

continued

BOX 2-1 Continued

2001–2004: NAS presentations about its activities within cooperative projects at four annual reviews in St. Petersburg of DOD/DTRA-supported research projects in Russia.

2001–2004: NAS agreements with the Departments of State, Health and Human Services, and Agriculture for assisting in the arrangement of biocooperation proposals and monitoring of projects in Russia.

2002–2008: Four NAS-RAS workshops in Moscow on terrorism, with bioterrorism as one of the priority topics. An NAS workshop proceedings published for each workshop.

2004: NAS organized small conference on diseases in Central Asia at Military Medical Research Academy in St. Petersburg.

2004: NAS report summarizing highlights of NAS-RAS cooperation over 50 years, with considerable attention to biocooperation.

2006: NAS report on the status of U.S.-Russian cooperation in biological sciences and biotechnology.

2007: NAS assessment of the DOD/DTRA program of cooperation with Russian institutions.

2013: RAS-NAS biosecurity training project at Novosibirsk State University for managers and scientists from Central Asia. RAS documentation prepared.

2013: NAS report, prepared in cooperation with the RAS, on the unique U.S.-Russian relationship in biological science and technology.

NOTE: More than 30 Russian offices, research centers, enterprises, and other facilities that were engaged in various aspects of biological science and technology hosted American participants during the aforementioned activities. Fifteen U.S. institutions hosted Russian specialists who participated in the collaborative activities. This disparity in opportunities for cross-ocean visits was due primarily to financial considerations. The activities were carried out during a time of financial austerity in Russia. Russian participants seldom had access to travel funds, while U.S participants were well supported by funding from U.S. government offices and by private foundations.

OPPORTUNITY FOR ENGAGING BIOPREPARAT

In 1995, the Director General of Russia's vast biological complex Biopreparat unexpectedly invited the NAS to participate in a meeting with his staff in the organization's secluded headquarters in Moscow, and a meeting was promptly arranged.[4] This director supervised a workforce that during Soviet times had numbered 50,000 specialists and support personnel working at three dozen research centers and monitoring laboratories, and at many production facilities throughout the former Soviet Union.

However, the military orientation of Biopreparat activities was changing. Some facilities had intensified their focus on production of biological pharmaceuticals that could outperform, if not outcompete, locally available health-enhancing products of questionable efficacy. Many products on the Russian market imported from India and several other distant countries were of questionable quality. A number of enterprises of Biopreparat had been struggling for years to find orders for their newly offered products from any source—at home or abroad; and the enterprises continued down paths of uncertainty.

The director was clearly concerned that other Russian organizations, but not *Biopreparat*, had found significant new income streams from benevolent Western organizations in exchange for access to their facilities in Russia. These Western customers, supported by their governments, apparently made no secret of their interest in redirection of the military capabilities of Russia to a focus on financially lucrative civilian-oriented activities. At the same time, new customers were gaining access to impressive scientific achievements of Russian laboratories and enterprises.

The director of Biopreparat, who was witnessing other Russian organizations respond to such new financial opportunities, was clearly interested in also receiving streams of international funding, whatever the motivations of potential customers. Buyers with cash in hand of any persuasion were welcomed. The director quickly offered a proposal for a meeting to join forces with the NAS along with other foreign organizations that shared his newly founded interest in promoting redirection of Russian scientists and engineers from military to civilian pursuits.

A tour of a few conference and display rooms of Biopreparat headquarters highlighted products intended for the civilian market. The host and his staff underscored that the Biopreparat management team was making progress in keeping its pharmaceutical plants in business, but the research laboratories were having particular difficulties. The director exuded confidence that the innovative capacity of the workforce could soon be a lynchpin for market success, particularly if Russian government officials who controlled financial matters found Biopreparat to be a better bet than other Russian companies for realizing profits in the marketplace.

The director then set forth his specific proposal—a jointly sponsored workshop hosted by Biopreparat at a location near Moscow. The 3-day affair would bring together American and Russian officials and scientists to identify opportunities for collaboration. The Americans could learn about the latent capabilities of his research institutions while he learned about interests of potential financial sponsors within foreign governments and within private industry. He undoubtedly knew that the idea of such a meeting was already being discussed in other circles in Moscow, but he wanted to claim some credit for the concept.

Agreement was quickly reached that such a workshop would be appropriate. He would arrange all administrative details—including ensuring that senior Russian officials would participate, while the interested U.S. organizations could enlist the support of industrialists and other financial sponsors of the workshop. He was confident that he could overcome the reluctance of Russian defense organizations to begin to unveil the Biopreparat establishment. He repeated several times that this complex included many activities ranging from research at the lead institution that was located 500 kilometers northeast of Moscow, to testing at closed facilities in downtown St. Petersburg, to analyzing biological samples in the forests of Siberia, to production activities on the banks of the Volga River, to production of pharmaceutical products in small industrial towns within several hours of Moscow. He added that the staffs of these facilities were not accustomed to reaching out beyond the perimeters of their facilities, and therefore the workshop would be a step in letting them know that it was acceptable for the world to be informed of their existence.

In short order, the workshop was held at a modest riverside retreat in the outskirts of Moscow. The gathering involved about 25 Russian and American researchers and research managers with extensive experience in the fields of virology, microbiology, and epidemiology. Several important Russian organizations were represented. Some participants were interested in activities within both production and research facilities. Others had spent their careers developing and overseeing implementation of policies for the handling of dangerous viruses and microbes.

The workshop, which involved formal presentations, barrages of questions, and quiet talks in nearby annexes, proved open and friendly. The dinners in the evenings and the walks in the forest during daylight were important opportunities for informal discussions. The event soon became a significant step for convening many subsequent U.S.-Russian events that gradually opened most of the biological landscape within Russia.[5]

Pathogens Initiative[6]

A number of collaborative activities that promoted political and scientific rapprochement quickly followed the aforementioned workshop. Congeniality and comradery suddenly became the order of the day as somewhat surprised Russian security and military personnel watched with interest. Many informal and formal events were documented within a landmark report published by the NAS, titled *Controlling Dangerous Pathogens: A Blueprint for U.S.-Russian Cooperation*. Of critical importance, the challenge for the U.S. government of enticing to the table former weapons-oriented scientists who were privy to long-held secrets throughout Russia's biological complex seemed to have been solved. The leadership of Biopreparat played a critical role in this transformation.[7]

Several NAS-sponsored activities following the workshop were of particular importance during the late 1990s, and they are described in detail in *Pathogens Initiative.* As an early step, the NAS, in cooperation with the RAS and Biopreparat, took the lead in organizing the aforementioned international scientific symposium in Kirov, where a central Russian military facility for biological research had long been located. Fifty participants, including representatives of 20 Russian organizations along with 15 foreigners, attended. The discussions covered epidemiology, rapid diagnostics, drugs, vaccines, antiviral preparations, and other topics of interest to the attendees and to the global biology community more broadly.

For the first time, Russian military scientists from the research institute in Kirov participated, although silently, in an event attended by 10 Americans and several invited scientists from other countries. In subsequent years, the conference attendees from Kirov assisted in arranging several other bilateral workshops on biological research issues near their home base. Also, alumni of service at the Kirov institute were occasionally encountered in leadership positions at other important research centers within Russia.

One of the most significant activities in opening the closed national security complex, which isolated Biopreparat researchers from western collaborators who were also interested in investigating activities involving highly dangerous pathogens in Russia, was the launching of eight pilot projects that were recommended by the NAS. Funding was provided by DOD/DTRA. Seven of the eight projects that are set forth in Box 2-2 produced impressive results given the modest level of funding provided by DOD/DTRA. These seven led to more ambitious U.S.-Russian efforts in expanding the scope of the projects, while encouraging the development of additional projects carried out on parallel tracks.

BROADENING THE SCOPE OF COOPERATIVE ACTIVITIES

Following the successful carrying out of the aforementioned pilot projects, the two Russian research centers where the projects had been undertaken became magnets for attracting U.S. scientists. VECTOR, which was cited in Box 2-2, adopted an open-door policy for some of its previously closed

---

BOX 2-2
Pilot Research Projects[8]

At the State Research Center of Virology and Biotechnology VECTOR in Koltsovo:

- Study of the prevalence, genotype distribution, and molecular variability of isolates of hepatitis C virus in the Asian part of Russia ($55,000).
- Study of the monkeypox virus genome ($55,000).
- Study of the genetic and serological diversity of hantavirus in the Asian part of Russia ($55,000).
- Development of an advanced diagnostic kit focused on opisthorchiasis in human patients ($55,000).
- Experimental studies of antiviral activities of glycyrrhyzic acid ($51,683) (not of interest to the U.S. collaborator but continued with the support of the host institution).

At the State Research Center for Applied Microbiology, Obolensk:

- Molecular-biological and immunochemical analysis of clinical strains of tuberculosis and mycobacteriosis ($138,000).
- Investigation of the immunological effectiveness of delivery in vivo of the Brucella main outer membrane protein by the anthrax toxin components ($61,500).
- Monitoring of anthrax ($55,000).

facilities, and in the early 2000s, the center became an important stop for many American virologists. Quickly following one another in their airline routes, American program managers—along with scientists and managers from other countries—arrived at the Novosibirsk airport for both long and short stints at VECTOR, where 2,000 employees, including 800 researchers, were at work. The range of their research activities was extensive. For example, they were isolating isolates of hepatitis B and C, developing new approaches in tracking the spread of viruses, developing technologies for manufacturing vaccines, and organizing stock-companies for sales and distribution of medical products.

Located in the heart of Siberia, VECTOR was led from its inception by Academician Lev Stepanovich Sandakchiev, a legendary research leader. By 2000, he personally welcomed visitors to facilities where the Russian researchers had seldom seen visitors from the United States and other countries. As a WHO Collaborating Center for Orthopoxvirus Diagnosis and a Center Repository for Variola Virus Strains and DNA, VECTOR at times hosted occasional visitors from Europe. However, in the early 2000s, such hosting exceeded by far the number of visitors and the openness of facilities than the international engagement in years past.[9]

The second center in Obolensk, also cited in Box 2-2, was located close to Moscow and had important facilities that American microbiologists from abroad began visiting as soon as the U.S.-Russian commitment to research on potentially dangerous pathogens began to unfold.

However, it did not have the mystique of a little-known isolated community. Of course, its facilities were also housed in secrecy due to the sensitivity of their activities, but as the facility opened up, the attraction of repetitive visits to a somewhat antiquated facility slowly waned.

Meanwhile, as to the feasibility of carrying out broader follow-on programs to the pilot projects set forth in Box 2-2, interest of potential financial sponsors in the United States was crucial. Again, DOD/DTRA immediately became a reliable source of support for transforming pronouncements and promises into reality. Also of significance was the preparedness of other U.S. funding organizations—including the Departments of State, Health and Human Services, and Agriculture—to eventually build on these early successes through cooperative programs on other bioresearch topics that they and additional interested American organizations selected during periodic consultations in Washington, D.C., and in Russia. The financial support by the U.S. government over a decade for developing and implementing projects of interest in Russia is set forth in Box 2-3.

BOX 2-3
Financial Support Provided to Russian Organizations
for Conduct of Biotech Projects as of 2013
When Cooperation Terminated[10]

DOD/DTRA	$36,500,000
DOD/DARPA	3,800,000
Department of Health and Human Services	30,700,000
Department of State (direct)	12,500,000
Department of State (through ISTC)	32,700,000
Department of Agriculture	23,400,000
Department of Energy	8,800,000
Environmental Protection Agency	6,800,000

On the Russian side, financial resources were in short supply. However, as long as program activities were carried out primarily in Russia, the local scientific community was ready and able to mobilize the talent, the facilities, and the enthusiasm necessary to have meaningful partnerships in the biological sciences for more than a decade. Thus, the scientific communities of the two countries undertook more than 200 collaborative projects sited in Russia of mutual interest in the biological sciences. During that period, the NAS received funds from a variety of U.S. government agencies and foundations to help guide and evaluate bioscience programs supported by the agencies. The total support of NAS activities for a decade, including strong support from DOD/DTRA, was about $4 million.

While the U.S. and Russian governments seemed intent on moving forward as rapidly as possible in promoting cooperation in the biological sciences, some observers were concerned about spreading knowledge of and capabilities for bioterrorism too widely. For example, in 2002 a prominent Russian scientist with a background in only unclassified activities highlighted how biological research activities could be used by fanatics or disenfranchised groups for blackmailing or promoting religious beliefs due to the following considerations:

- Many laboratories and pharmaceutical facilities had the capability to produce dangerous biological agents.
- With development of the internet, access to information on the culture of viruses and microorganisms and the production of toxins had become simple.
- Obtaining a pathogenic strain of a microorganism or a virus is easy.
- Bioweapons are effective in very small doses, with easy concealment, and could be used on individual targets or for mass infections.
- Society is neither technically nor psychologically ready for bioterrorism.

Such concerns were far from new. But the Russian scientist apparently believed that the simplicity of spreading deadly biological agents should be widely discussed to gain support for research that could counter the threat.[11]

As interest in bilateral cooperation expanded, DOD/DTRA asked the NAS to conduct scientific reviews of research projects proposed by Russian institutes for financial support. More than 80 proposals were reviewed, with the average cost for a project if it were implemented being about $300,000. Many were considered by NAS experts to be very promising in contributing to the advancement of science.

At the same time, for each proposal the reviewers had a redline. Did the proposal come too close to providing a technology that would be useful in developing a weapons capability? About 10 percent of the proposals fell on the wrong side of that line and were rejected.

As to the 90 percent, about one-half of the proposals were rejected as not being of particular scientific interest. Most of the remainder were then approved in principle for implementation. However, many required significant modifications and resubmission.

After all this work, DOD/DTRA decided to put aside NAS recommendations and established another process for selecting proposals for implementation. This process began with on-site visits by DOD/DTRA scientists to Russian facilities, where topics for proposals would be discussed and funding decisions would be made. The NAS efforts were not completely wasted, however. They gave DOD/DTRA confidence that there were many ideas among Russian scientists that were worthy of support, and some of the original submissions to the NAS subsequently reappeared as approved DOD/DTRA projects. The DOD/DTRA was the first of several departments and agencies to request the NAS to assess project proposals in the biological sciences. Other agencies often relied on the views of the NAS on the importance of projects or the details of the proposals.

As indicated in Box 2-3, many sound proposals received by different U.S. departments and agencies were supported. The appendixes of several NAS reports identified many of the more than 200 research projects that were financed by the U.S. government during 2000–2010 at a cost to the U.S. government of more than $160 million. This was a relatively small, but a significant, component of the $1 billion investment by U.S. and Russian organizations in bio-engagement activities in Russia from 1995 to 2010. The U.S. institutions paid for most of the direct personnel costs, and the Russian institutions covered all of the other costs, including extensive indirect expenses that at times involved providing new facilities for the projects.[12]

In a broader sense, the following suggestions, which are set forth in the aforementioned 2007 report, proposed four pillars for countering infectious diseases in Russia. These activities had a modest impact on Russian approaches in preventing the spread of infectious diseases.

- **Pillar 1 – Improving Surveillance and Response:** Many upgraded State Epidemiology Surveillance Centers for surveillance diagnosis, analysis, and communication of infectious disease episodes at the oblast and local levels were established. Integration of Russia's anti-plague network into the national public health surveillance system and then into the global system was not achieved. Nevertheless, the information flow between the research centers of the anti-plague network and the other research centers in Russia improved.
- **Pillar 2 – Meeting Pathogen Research Challenges:** Financial support was to a considerable degree focused on carefully selected research groups that had the potential to become centers of scientific excellence. Upgraded laboratory facilities and equipment for appropriate infectious disease–related research at selected laboratories became commonplace throughout many areas of the country.
- **Pillar 3 – Promise of Biotechnology:** An effective business environment that encouraged foreign and national investment in biotechnology activities in Russia was not achieved. While government procurement policies that favored high-quality Russian products over imported products at times were helpful, many possible market niches for Russian firms were not exploited.
- **Pillar 4 – Human Resources Base:** While many postdoctoral scientists were encouraged to remain in Russia as practicing scientists,

mentoring programs that prepared them for positions of leadership in fields focused on control of infectious diseases were not commonplace. Advanced training programs that expanded the competence of specialists in fields related to infectious diseases, particularly fields involving multidisciplinary challenges, were limited.[13]

In further summing up some of the positive impacts of U.S.-Russian cooperation in the biological sciences, an NAS report in 2013 highlighted the following developments:

- The adoption of unique research approaches has been frequent, with research findings of joint efforts being significant.
- Transparency and insights about accomplishments and future plans has increased greatly with a dramatic reduction in suspicions about inappropriate intentions of political leaders in the two countries.
- Following a long period of hesitation, entrepreneurial investors in the two countries have taken initial steps to develop joint commercial opportunities.
- Effective approaches have been developed through working together to ensure biosafety when (a) handling dangerous pathogens encountered during disease surveillance, (b) reducing agricultural pests and pathogens, and (c) reducing environmental problems.[14]

Also, the same report highlighted the importance of easing visa problems in traveling in both directions, effectively addressing tax and customs issues, protecting intellectual property, adopting proper procedures for international shipment of specimens, and complying with export control requirements.[15]

NEAR-TERM IMPACTS OF THE BIODEFENSE PROGRAM

In 2007, the NAS carried out an evaluation of the impacts of the biodefense program supported by the DOD/DTRA in Russia. Specific changes in the region—primarily in Russia but also to a limited extent in other former states of the Soviet Union—included the following:

- Unprecedented transparency at dozens of important facilities with dual-use capabilities that had not previously been open to foreign specialists.

- Dismantlement and/or conversion of production and research facilities established to support biological weapons activities, including transformation to civilian activities of more than a dozen important components of the weapons-oriented Biopreparat complex.
- Redirection to civilian pursuits of hundreds of biological scientists, engineers, and technical personnel who were formerly engaged in defense programs.
- Attraction and retention of hundreds of younger specialists working in basic science and in the fields of public health and agriculture.
- Adoption by local institutions of standard international approaches to project management and fiscal accountability.
- Participation in scientific conferences and training programs abroad by specialists from the region who had not previously traveled abroad.
- Increased publication by local scientists in peer-reviewed international journals of research findings, which demonstrated their new capabilities to participate in international scientific activities.
- Enhanced quality of local research projects and technology transfer activities that have taken advantage of the experience and expertise of international collaborators.
- Improved biosecurity and biosafety at biological research institutions, particularly for consolidation and physical protection of dangerous pathogen strains.
- Opening and sharing of local databases with international collaborators.
- Construction and equipping of modern research, public health, and agricultural facilities where activities of interest to international partners are carried out.
- Development of local regulations and related training programs for the safety and security of biological materials and good laboratory practices.[16]

LESSONS LEARNED

Lessons learned of interest to governments and managers of Russian bioscience facilities during the preparations and implementation of proposals included the following:

- U.S.-Russian cooperation in the biosciences as well as in other areas may at times resemble a foreign assistance relationship but should evolve into a partnership, although equitable sharing of direct costs may be difficult to arrange. However, the *goal* of sharing direct costs, thereby reducing U.S. dominance in determining project objectives, is important in sustaining long-term relationships.
- Support or at least acceptance by all concerned government agencies in both countries of the proposed collaboration in a specific area is an important first step in launching a project.
- The time commitments of key interlocutors, including the project managers and key overseers, should be clear from the outset.
- Cooperation should build on the mutual strengths of the two countries, and continuing ongoing activities should usually be on solid footing.
- Importance of up-front planning, including pilot efforts, prior to implementation of significant activities cannot be overemphasized.
- Development of strategies for obtaining long-term support deserves priority.
- Narrow nonproliferation objectives are of less importance than building capacity for addressing biological challenges over the long term.
- Early involvement of users of applied research results in the research planning and implementation is very important.
- All aspects of equipment selection, use, and maintenance need to be given early consideration when collaboration requires new equipment. Also, compliance with local quality assurance environmental requirements needs special attention.[17]

Lessons learned by research scientists included the following:

- Too often interested parties incorrectly assume that government approval of a collaborative project means that financial support will be provided by one or both of the governments until the project is completed.
- Key collaborators for individual projects should have common interests and capabilities that are well matched.
- In-person joint planning and review throughout implementation of the project is important.

- Open communications that facilitate access to primary data, interim results, and modifications of research approaches are important throughout project implementation.
- Joint projects are most interesting for both researchers and policy officials when they are oriented toward application of results.
- If grants are obtained to fund specific research challenges, the activities should be focused on the themes set forth in the grant applications.
- Special efforts may be needed to involve investigators who are in the early stages of their careers. They may bring fresh insights to projects that might otherwise be stymied by out-of-date concepts.
- The more institutions involved in a joint project, the more important is agreement on administrative arrangements. One-on-one institutional arrangements may work better and more efficiently than broader arrangements for a single project.
- There may be requirements for special facilities and procedures to accommodate new lines of research, and these issues must be resolved before the project is initiated.
- Professional rewards from joint projects can be highly visible, and they may encourage others to engage in international programs.[18]

BROADENING INTERNATIONAL COLLABORATION AND THE WAY AHEAD

In 2008, at the height of U.S.-Russian collaboration in determining biological research priorities, Russian colleagues reported the following research findings that opened important doors for long-term collaboration:

The commercial breeding of the rare palm civets for their meat was the source of severe acute respiratory syndrome caused by SARS coronavirus in China. The Chinese recently started eating palm civet meat and breeding the animals, and civets frequently carry the coronavirus. Researchers have discovered that a random deletion of an insignificant portion of the gene encoding a key protein (less than 0.1 percent of the genome) and several nucleotide substitutions made this coronavirus infectious for humans. When consumption of civet meat and commercial breeding of the animals were halted, human contact with these animals also stopped, as did the epidemics caused by the coronavirus in question.[19]

Given the common interests in coronavirus infections among biological scientists throughout the world, it is not surprising that in 2020, a relatively low point in U.S.-Russian political relations, the U.S. and Russian academies gave priority to related efforts to address the related challenges of the global spread of COVID-19, as indicated at the beginning of this chapter.

Joint U.S.-Russian academy efforts to reach out to biological institutions and scientists in other countries, either within the context of activities of international organizations or simply bilaterally, were repeatedly considered during implementation of bilateral activities discussed in this report.

An important step in the formalization of joint efforts directed to activities in other countries was taken in 2013 when the NAS and the Siberian Branch of the RAS joined efforts to help strengthen biosecurity activities in four countries in Central Asia. Scientists from the United States and Russia carried out separate but coordinated visits to Kazakhstan, Uzbekistan, Kyrgyzstan, and Tajikistan, where they consulted with leading biological research scientists, biosecurity specialists, and government officials. The Siberian Branch, in cooperation with the NAS, then organized a workshop on the campus of Novosibirsk State University for specialists from these four countries to increase the familiarity of the specialists with recent developments in upgrading biosecurity arrangements. Unfortunately, on the eve of the workshop, the U.S. government, which planned to cover the travel costs for American participants in the workshop, placed a ban on all travel to Russia for political reasons. When the travel ban was announced, the leader of the NAS team was in China, but he was allowed to continue his travel to Novosibirsk. The Russian partners rearranged the program, and they and the American specialist performed double duty for the workshop.

Globalization of travel and trade, emerging infectious diseases, and widening threats of bioterrorism have heighted the urgency of harnessing the scientific and technological abilities of all countries, in a united counterattack on pervasive and persistent disease agents that can wreak human and economic havoc. Clearly, Russia should be on the frontlines of the global efforts along with the United States to help prevent and contain outbreaks of diseases at home and abroad.

As bilateral cooperation evolved and provided the base for outreach to other countries, mistrust on both sides that had hampered cooperation in the biological sciences during the cold war diminished. The importance of engagement activities not only provided a scientific return but also helped build confidence internationally in the importance of collaborative research and related efforts in bioscience and biotechnology between former adversaries.[20]

The United States and Russia have different sets of international contacts that collectively provide good global coverage of important research that could lead to significant discoveries in the biological sciences. Many developing countries have few scientists who can address rapidly the emergence of new biological challenges. For them to be able to draw on both U.S. and Russian mentors can avoid waste of time and money and reduce international misunderstanding and confusion.

VIEWS FROM THE FRONTIERS OF BIOLOGY

An American biologist with experience in collaboration with colleagues across Russia underlined the importance of *global* surveillance as follows:

We must have the will to accomplish the important task of very early awareness and response to naturally emerging and intentional diseases, although we do not know exactly how to accomplish this goal. We must watch the spots where the animals, humans, and bugs collide. We now have the technical tools and know-how to implement the necessary public health infrastructure for surveillance and response nearly anywhere around the globe. The world has become too small and the potential for harm too great to stand idle. Technology allows implementation today. We must not let politics or borders stand in the way. Working together across national boundaries on one of the most challenging and important human security issues of our time will not only protect our citizens from natural disease but also contribute to building understanding and even trust that will reduce the likelihood that intentional outbreaks will negatively impact any of our populations.[21]

Directly supporting the previous observations is a statement by another advocate of global networking.

In the long term, it is the networks of scientists around the globe that will provide the major payoffs from collaboration at the national, regional, and global levels. It is essential that both American and Russian biological scientists have seats in these networks. Rewards are often measured in terms of research discoveries, development of new products, improved health and agricultural services, and prevention of misuse of biotechnologies. While these indicators of success are important, the major payoff from new-found friendships across the ocean, an outcome that can last decades, is the network of scientists who are interested in working together through visits, conference attendance, e-mails, or other means during many years of their professional careers. There is no better assurance than the respect and camaraderie surrounding such friendships that the life sciences will indeed be used for the betterment of the global population.[22]

NOTES

1. Netesov, S. V. 2009. "Emerging Viral Infections in the Asian Part of Russia," in *Countering Terrorism: Biological Agents, Transportation Networks, and Energy Systems, Summary of a U.S.-Russian Workshop*. Washington, DC: The National Academies Press, p. 93.

2. Franz, D. R. 2014. "Engaging the States of the Former Soviet Union in Health Security, Biosecurity, and Bioterrorism." *Biosecurity and Bioterrorism: Biodefense Strategy, Practice, and Science* 12(2): 367.

3. NRC (National Research Council). 2007. *The Biological Threat Reduction Program of the Department of Defense*. Washington, DC: The National Academies Press, p. 15.

4. Schweitzer, G. E. 2000. *Swords into Market Shares*, Washington, DC: Joseph Henry Press, p. 189.

5. Schweitzer, G. E. 2004. *Scientists, Engineers and Track-Two Diplomacy*. Washington, DC: The National Academies Press, p. 50.

6. NRC. 1997. *Controlling Dangerous Pathogens: a Blueprint for U.S.-Russian Cooperation*. Washington, DC: The National Academies Press.

7. Op. cit., Schweitzer, *Swords*, p. 189; NRC, *Pathogens*.

8. Op. cit., Schweitzer, *Scientists*, p. 52.

9. *State Research Center of Virology and Biotechnology "Vector."* Moscow: Ministry of Public Health and Social Development, 2004.

10. NRC. 2013. *The Unique U.S.-Russian Relationship in Biological Science and Biotechnology*. Washington, DC: The National Academies Press, p. 213.

11. Morenkov, O. S. 2009. "Bioterrorism: A View from the Side," in *Russian Views on Countering Terrorism during Eight Years of Dialogue: Extracts from Proceedings of Four U.S.-Russian Workshops*. Washington, DC: The National Academies Press, p. 23.

12. Op. cit., *The Unique U.S.-Russian Relationship*, p. 2, and Appendix C; op. cit., *Biological Threat Reduction Program*, Appendix F.

13. NRC. 2006. *Bioscience and Biotechnology in Russia: Controlling Diseases and Enhancing Security*. Washington, DC: The National Academies Press, p. 4–7.

14. Ibid., p. 4.

15. Ibid.

16. Op. cit., *Biological Threat Reduction Program*, p. 2.

17. Ibid., p. 103.

18. Ibid., p. 104.

19. Netesov, S. V., and N. A. Markovich. 2009. "Emerging Viral Infections in the Asian Part of Russia," in *Countering Terrorism: Biological Agents, Transportation. Networks, and Energy Systems: Summary of a U.S.-Russian Workshop.* Washington, DC: The National Academies Press, p. 91.
20. Op. cit., *Biological Threat Reduction Program*, p. 35.
21. Franz, D. R. 2009. "Disease Surveillance and International Biosecurity," in *Countering Terrorism, Biological Agents, Transportation Networks, and Energy Systems: Summary of a U.S-Russian Workshop.* Washington, DC: The National Academies Press, p. 78.
22. Op. cit., *Unique U.S.-Russian Relationship*, p. 121.

Russian-American Conference on Medical Challenges in Central Asia and Other Similar Areas of Concern held in 2004 at the Russian Military-Medical Academy in St. Petersburg. During the conference the Russian participants praised American General Russ Zajtchuk (ret) of Rush University Medical Center for his long-term support of the Academy.
Source: Photograph provided by the hosts for unlimited distribution.

Participants in RAS-NAS Workshop on Biological Safety and Security Held in Novosibirsk, Russia, in 2014 for Specialists from Central Asia.
Source: Photograph provided by Novosibirsk State University for unlimited distribution.

3

Radiological Challenges:
Security, Sources, Waste Sites, and Disposal

In Moscow during 1993, a cesium-137 source was placed in an arm-chair killing one person; and in 1995, another cesium-137 source was discovered in a public park also in Moscow. In Chechnya during 2002, a Russian army team used robots to retrieve two stolen sources. Then in the Russian Far East in 2003, thieves stripped off the metal casings of radioactive thermal generators at three lighthouses.

– NAS report, 2007[1]

The world has not yet given adequate attention to the dangers of misuse of radioactive sources, spent nuclear fuel, and radioactive waste to make radiological devices. The greatest consequences of detonation of such a device are public fear, potentially enormous cleanup costs, and consequent economic losses. There is essentially no barrier to terrorists obtaining radioactive material. Three new inter-academy projects will be undertaken to address this issue.

– Joint statement of the presidents of the NAS and the RAS, 2002[2]

While protecting well-known storage, assembly, and operational locations for radioactive material is very important, terrorists are often on the move searching along the way for any type of material that could cause damage. Therefore, security specialists should be aware that terrorists may come upon radiological material in unusual places, which are not designated or known as facilities having such material.

– NAS report, 2019[3]

BROAD AGENDA OF ACTIVITIES

This chapter addresses the extensive cooperation of the National Academy of Sciences (NAS) and a wide array of Russian partners in addressing many nuclear-related challenges, with most activities carried out in Russia. The Russian Academy of Sciences (RAS) was involved in almost all of these activities, serving as a partner or as a facilitator in arranging contacts and visits with approval of many Russian government agencies. Issues concerning arms control are not included in this report. Box 3-1 highlights many of the most important activities.

BOX 3-1
Radiological Security Activities

1997: NAS report on nuclear proliferation concerns in the former Soviet Union.

1999: NAS report *Protecting Nuclear Weapons Material in Russia*, with visits to facilities in Moscow, Obninsk, Dubna, Podolsk, Dmitrovgrad, Los Alamos, Albuquerque, Oak Ridge, and Livermore.

1999–2009: Establishment and continuation of the Inter-Academy Committee on Terrorism, with initial emphasis on nuclear issues: a series of four workshops in Moscow with visits to nuclear facilities in Moscow and other Russian cities and towns.

2002: NAS-RAS workshop in Moscow on nuclear nonproliferation, with visits to offices and facilities in Moscow, Sergiev Posad, Gatchina, Yekaterinburg, Zarechny, and Washington, D.C.

2003: NAS-RAS workshop in Moscow on spent nuclear fuel with visits to facilities in Mayak, Chelyabinsk, Ozersk, Dmitrovgrad, and Moscow.

2005: NAS-RAS workshop on a proposal for an international spent nuclear fuel facility with a visit to facilities in Krasnokamensk.

2006: NAS report on long-term nuclear security with visits to facilities in Moscow, Obninsk, Podolsk, Elektrostal, Gatchina, Oak Ridge, and the Y-12 security complex in Tennessee.

2007: NAS report on combating radiological terrorism with visits to facilities in Moscow, Sergiev Posad, Yekaterinburg, and Zarechny.

BOX 3-1 Continued

2008: NAS-RAS workshop in Vienna on a proposed international fuel facility, with a visit to the International Atomic Energy Agency headquarters.

2018: NAS-RAS workshop in Helsinki on violent extremism and radiological security.

2019: NAS-RAS workshop in Moscow on violent extremism and radiological security, with a visit to the radiological waste facility in Sergiev Posad.

2021: Planning for the third NAS-RAS workshop in Moscow on violent extremism and radiological security.

DETERIORATION OF STRICT SECURITY THROUGHOUT RUSSIA'S NUCLEAR COMPLEX

As Russia was slowly recovering from the economic catastrophe that engulfed the country during the late 1990s following the breakup of the Soviet Union into 15 independent states, the U.S. Departments of State, Defense, and Energy (DOE) encouraged the NAS to work with the RAS and appropriate Russian research centers in assessing the security of nuclear material in Russia. The U.S. departments provided significant financial support for field assessments, workshops, and studies. They were concerned that although intergovernmental programs were having some effect on upgrading the security at many Russian facilities, the gravity of the threat involving nuclear material was actually increasing.

The continuing decline in the Russian economy had severely affected the economic well-being of Russian government officials, nuclear specialists, and workers who had access to direct-use material. While such material must be closely guarded even in the best of economic times, economic deprivation had increased the likelihood of such material disappearing from Russian facilities as families throughout the country struggled to meet everyday needs.[4]

At the same time, expanded access to Russian facilities by American participants in intergovernmental programs provided new insights into the vast Russian nuclear complex. More extensive illegal diversion of material and more pervasive weaknesses of protection systems than had been anticipated were uncovered. The Russian government also recognized the magnitude of the problem, as the deputy minister for atomic energy announced that there had been 28 incidents of illegal access to nuclear material at facilities throughout the nuclear complex between 1992 and 1995. Other officials acknowledged continuation of attempted thievery in subsequent years. Also, NAS specialists were told by managers of several important Russian facilities that penetration of their security systems had become a major concern.[5]

As an example of NAS involvement, in 1999 a team of American and Russian experts visited 13 Russian facilities where tons of nuclear material were available for a variety of purposes. The primary focus of the visit was to ascertain the status of the materials protection, control, and accountability (MPC&A) activities at the facilities. Particular attention was given to possible weaknesses in accountability, which was suspected of falling short in many respects. Soon thereafter, other NAS teams visiting Russia heard reports from managers of additional facilities that the number of attempted thefts of dangerous material continued to be of concern. In response to such reports, the Russian government required many facilities to tighten their control of nuclear material; and the number of attempted thefts during subsequent years dropped significantly.[6]

Also in 1999, the NAS advised the DOE that although the priorities in the MPC&A programs being supported were generally consistent with the most urgent needs in protecting nuclear material, the following issues required prompt attention:

- There was very slow progress in installing and putting into operation material accountancy systems at Russian sites—including even the basic step of ensuring complete and accurate inventories of nuclear material.
- With several important exceptions, only limited progress had been made in efforts to consolidate direct-use material at a variety of sites into fewer buildings to reduce the number of locations that required the highest level of security.
- Neither DOE nor Russian institutions had developed strategies to ensure the long-term sustainability of the upgraded systems for MPC&A that had been established.
- Inadequate progress had been made in providing appropriate transport systems and vehicles to ensure that direct-use material was secure during shipments within and between sites.

Thus, the remaining tasks were considered "huge" within both the U.S. and Russian governments.[7]

In 2005, the NAS issued its third assessment of the DOE program, which was designed to assist Russian counterparts in the upgrading of MPC&A systems. The report strongly supported many of the pioneering efforts of DOE. At the same time, there were important findings that called for additional actions. In general, these findings, supplemented with statements by many Russian security officials, indicated that security enhancements installed through the DOE program probably played an important role in significantly reducing the number of attempted thefts of dangerous nuclear material from Russian facilities. But additional efforts were in order. Among the findings in the report calling for future security measures were the following:

- Russian experts remained concerned about terrorist attacks on nuclear facilities focused primarily on sabotage, which could be prevented through guards and perimeter defenses. However, insufficient priority had been given to using modern electronic and optical methods to assist in preventing "insider" theft of material when the economy was in a very depressed state.
- Weapons-usable material was not as well protected from outsider penetration as it should have been in view of the increasingly aggressive terrorist activities within Russia.
- In determining activities at specific Russian facilities, DOE representatives usually dominated the discussions with Russian counterparts about upgrade priorities and approaches. An administrative culture that regarded Russian counterparts as "contractors with checklists" had emerged within DOE.
- Even taking into account progress in many aspects of protecting materials of concern during a decade of cooperation, the overall program had moved slowly in bringing hundreds of tons of weapons-usable material under greater control.
- The practice of relying on large DOE contracts with Russian counterpart organizations that had originally been adopted was replaced with the adoption of small contracts due to complaints by the U.S. Congress about the ease of misuse of funds. The increase in the number of contracts that expanded administrative processes delayed implementation of important activities by many months.

- Accountability of the amounts, locations, and uses of nuclear material continued to require more attention.

A key concern of the report was the lack of appreciation of the importance of *indigenization* of the program, with the following overarching components:

- An unwavering political commitment by the Russian government from the political to the institutional levels for maintaining a high level of proven security measures in protecting nuclear material.
- Adequate Russian resources at the facility level to fulfill such a commitment.
- Approaches to installing security systems that were not only technically sound but fully embraced by Russian managers and specialists.[8] Box 3-2 highlights lessons learned in effectively addressing indigenization.

Most of the foregoing changes based on lessons learned were, in time, incorporated into MPC&A programs that were supported by the DOE in many areas of Russia. However, these changes remain instructive when addressing large foreign-financed technical assistance programs in other countries that are attempting to quickly take charge of their own industrial development challenges.

TENS OF THOUSANDS OF POTENT IONIZING RADIATION SOURCES IN USE AND OUT OF USE IN RUSSIA

While DOE was making good progress in upgrading its programs to improve security of weapons-usable material at many Russian facilities, the NAS began to consider other aspects of radiological security in response to new requests from DOE. Of special concern was the handling of ionizing radiation sources (IRSs) for a variety of purposes in the medical, agricultural, food, geophysical, energy, and industrial fields.

For decades, the International Atomic Energy Agency (IAEA) had warned the world that packing conventional explosives together with radioactive material and detonating such a radiological dispersal device to kill and/or terrorize people—the dirty bomb scenario—were within the means of some terrorist groups. This warning was particularly strong when focusing on radioactive material in Russia. In addition to the large inventory

BOX 3-2
Lessons Learned about
Indigenization of Cooperative Efforts[9]

- Emphasize the importance of MPC&A at the highest political level of Russia.
- Prior to initiating MPC&A projects, obtain assurances at ministry and institute levels that the upgrade programs will be sustained.
- Involve institute personnel to the fullest extent possible in determining use of available funds.
- Emphasize prompt training of local specialists.
- Reward institutes that make good progress in upgrading MPC&A systems by giving them preference in participating in future projects.
- Encourage establishment of new income streams for support of the program in future years.
- Rely increasingly on domestically produced and locally available equipment for fulfilling MPC&A tasks.
- Increase U.S. funding for the program but ensure that the counterpart contribution grows at an even faster rate.
- Expand the use of Russian equipment and services while encouraging counterparts to increase the capability to provide high-quality equipment and associated warrants and services.
- Use Russian specialists from institutes with successful programs to replace Americans working in institutes, which had less advanced capabilities.
- Rely increasingly on Russian specialists to replace Americans in directing training activities.
- Encourage the Moscow Engineering Physics Institute to attract students to participate in MPC&A training activities by also offering them broader industrial security training that would increase their employment opportunities at a later stage in their careers.
- Give greater attention to developing personal commitments of Russian managers, specialists, and guard forces for ensuring installation and operation of high-quality MPC&A systems.
- Increase opportunities for Russian input in preparing statements of work at specific sites.

of inadequately protected uranium and plutonium that could be used in nuclear weapons, many hundreds of Russian institutions throughout the country had IRSs or other forms of nuclear material that could become components of dirty bombs.

After years of frustration among nuclear specialists within both the United States and Russia about the lack of adequate attention being given to dangerous IRSs, in 2006 DOE requested the NAS to assess the threat posed locally and internationally by IRSs in Russia. The most common uses of IRSs included the applications set forth in Box 3-3.

During the early 2000s, NAS specialists learned many details about the problems Russia had inherited from the former Soviet Union in controlling a very large number of *potent* IRSs throughout the country. They probably numbered in the tens of thousands. The Mayak Production Association was the leading Russian manufacturer of IRSs—for domestic uses and for export. Many of the uncontrolled IRSs had been produced at Mayak and were then sold or given to hundreds of organizations.

There were many concerns over the control of IRSs. A particularly important focus was the hundreds of radioisotope thermoelectric generators located in the northern and central reaches of the country, with formidable logistics required to locate and retrieve those that were no longer needed. As to less potent sources, tens of thousands of IRSs were discovered in hundreds of institutions, enterprises, hospitals, and other facilities—including many abandoned buildings—located within reach of skilled criminals. In addition,

---

BOX 3-3
Uses of High-Risk Radioactive Sources[10]

- Radioisotope thermoelectric generators
- Sterilization and food irradiation
- Blood irradiation
- Single-beam teletherapy
- Multi-beam teletherapy
- Industrial radiography
- Calibration
- High- and medium-dose-rate brachytherapy
- Well logging
- Level and conveyor gauges

there were reports of IRSs being discovered in open fields in central Russia in the spring as the snow melted.

Reliable estimates or even approximate estimates of the number of IRSs being used, in storage, or in an abandoned state in Russia had never existed. The total may have been more than 1 million IRSs when Russia became an independent country. Thousands were believed to have been of sufficient strength to be of considerable concern to the IAEA, which has long classified IRSs according to their potency.

Russian and American participants in an NAS-RAS project during 2006 visited a variety of Russian facilities to improve their understanding of the state of security surrounding the possession of IRSs. Their reports on visits to five facilities included the following observations:

- Four cesium-137 sources of about 5,000 curies each were maintained in an unprotected room of a poorly guarded facility adjacent to a forest.
- Another facility had 6,000 sources of various kinds. In one building, a flimsy door opened into a room with two irradiators that used cobalt-60 and cesium-137 sources. In an adjacent building, gamma-type irradiators could be wheeled out in a hand cart.
- A dormant facility retained 36 sources of cobalt-60 with a total activity of 20,000 curies. The storage room was on the ground floor opening directly onto the courtyard. The fire and security alarms were outdated with externally exposed cables.
- A facility containing 27 sources of cobalt-60 and 15 sources of cesium-137 was located within 300 meters of a metro station, a school, and apartments. There were no restrictions on entering the portion of the building containing the sources. The containment room was subjected to surface and subsoil water, which had weakened the strength of the walls and floor of the building.
- Forty-two sources of various types, which had not been used for years, were located in a crumbling factory building. The guard force was not professionally trained. The facility had no fence and did not connect to the municipal alarm system. On the site were several commercial firms, which had no legal relationship to the storage facility, which was on the verge of bankruptcy.[11]

Based on the foregoing observations together with numerous comparable testimonials by Russian experts, the NAS recommended several immediate steps to help strengthen the security surrounding the possession of IRSs:

- The DOE's limited program of quick security fixes should be expedited. Of particular importance was the end-of-life-cycle management of IRSs that were no longer wanted, including many that had been simply abandoned.
- The DOE should develop a comprehensive plan for working with Russian counterparts to reduce the overall risk and consequences of radiological terrorism.
- Cooperation should be developed within the context of the overall Russian program for ensuring adequate life-cycle management of IRSs throughout the country and should take into account activities of other external partners.[12]

Adding to the urgency of reducing the likelihood of successful terrorist activities, which included dissemination of IRSs, were the observations of a team of collaborating Russian experts. They were concerned about (a) near-term radiation effects of inadequately protected IRSs on the population within hours or days, and (b) delayed effects due to prolonged irradiation resulting from environmental contamination. These experts also warned about social, economic, political, psychological, and demographic consequences to society, including the following:

- Unnoticed long-term health effects on the general population, contamination of habitable structures, and loss of property values.
- Costs of both immediate cleanup and long-term radiation-reduction measures to protect the population.
- Population movement away from contaminated areas.
- Withdrawal from the economy of activities in contaminated areas.
- Negative attitudes toward nuclear power development.
- Long-term aquifer contamination.[13]

Russian colleagues also explored the feasibility and possible consequences of the following five scenarios involving the possible acquisition of radioactive material and then the launching of attacks by terrorists:

- Planting a radioactive source containing cobalt-60 in a subway car.
- Detonation in the subway system of a strontium-90–based dirty bomb.
- Dispersion of cesium-137–impregnated material over an urban area.

- Detonation of a dirty bomb based on americium-241 in or near a large city.
- Liquid dispersion of a radiation source over a segment of an asphalt road leading to a major highway that would extend the contamination picked up on the tires of vehicles to other streets.[14]

Another report concluded that IRSs are at times found in scrap metal, many sources are discovered in vehicles and transport containers, and theft is a common event.[15]

SECURITY AT MANY RADIOLOGICAL WASTE SITES IN RUSSIA

Beginning with the challenge in assessing the extent and impact of the debris from the catastrophe at Chernobyl, for many years collaboration in assessing the collection, handling, and disposition of radioactive waste became an important activity of the NAS and the RAS. Three months after the Chernobyl disaster in 1986, the NAS was one of several sponsors of an international conference in a hastily erected temporary shelter a few kilometers from the scene of the explosion. The focus of the conference was on the extent and impact of environmental contamination. The NAS played an important role in inviting carefully chosen American experts to attend the conference and also in identifying appropriate participants for follow-up studies that continued for decades.[16]

The many movies and books highlighting deterioration of wooded areas and elimination of animals and insects that had inhabited the forests soon encouraged greater international attention to ecological impacts. The early NAS emphasis on ecological impacts helped facilitate NAS-RAS cooperation involving a variety of colleagues from Moscow and Obninsk.[17]

In more recent years, the NAS and the RAS sponsored a series of workshops on radiological challenges, commissioning preparation of reports on the disposal of radioactive wastes resulting from the growth of the nuclear industry in Russia. During the early 2000s, the focus was on the conditions and some of the practices at 15 of 27 well-known Russian waste sites. The NAS, together with the RAS, invited many Russian scientific leaders to prepare technical essays on activities at the sites.[18] Several Russian scientists who participated were familiar with U.S. approaches, having visited the proposed disposal site in Yucca Mountain, Nevada.[19]

There were subsequent inter-academy activities directed to the challenges of safe and efficient disposal of radioactive waste. Several meetings and workshops sponsored by the NAS and the RAS addressed the possibility of a Russian initiative to establish an international waste repository for spent nuclear fuel in Russia, which is discussed below. More recently, an important focus during inter-academy discussions has been on new technologies for expanding deep disposal, upgrading radioactive waste containers, and introducing innovative approaches for temporary storage of waste. Throughout this time, an important partner for the NAS has been the Russian enterprise RADON, which leads Russia's national effort to provide safe storage and processing of nonmilitary nuclear waste.

To set the stage for many activities, in 2003 the NAS and the RAS launched a series of workshops on the handling of radioactive waste. The first workshop was titled "End Points for High-Level Radioactive Waste in Russia and the United States." One area of particular interest to American experts was the Russian program to chemically process most of its solid radioactive waste before burial. A related area of special interest was Russian experience in deep-well injection of large amounts of low-level and intermediate-level waste generated by several radiochemical facilities. A third development of global interest was the dumping of liquid radioactive waste into Lake Karachay and the ensuing Techa Reservoir Cascade adjacent to the Mayak industrial facility.[20]

In view of the continuing international interest in the environmental problems in and near Mayak, a few comments on the situation in that area are offered. Eight industrial reservoirs for liquid radioactive wastes were established to support defense program operations, and these reservoirs had many long-term impacts. Also in 1957, a leak at a liquid radioactive holding tank in the area resulted in the creation of the well-known East Urals Radioactive Trace, with two reservoirs used to store medium-level wastes. Next a man-made reservoir was built to store low-level liquid waste. Then unexpectedly, the wind dispersed radioactive substances from an exposed shoreline.

Finally by 2009, program objectives had been established as follows:

- Reduce and ultimately halt all discharges of liquid radioactive waste.
- Eliminate the most radiologically hazardous reservoirs.
- Ensure safe operations of the Techa Cascade of reservoirs.
- Reduce the volume and radioactivity levels of high-level waste stored in holding tanks.[21]

Turning to many other waste challenges throughout the country, the following objectives were given high priority:

- Consolidating excessive nuclear materials in a few reliably protected facilities.
- Developing and refining technologies for safe and efficient defueling, dismantling, and disposing of decommissioned nuclear-powered submarines.
- Transporting by secure means spent nuclear fuel between facilities.
- Developing standards for highly durable waste forms.
- Immobilizing different types of high-level wastes.
- Developing unified objectives for selection of geological media and sites for high-level wastes for long-term storage and disposal.
- Promoting research on methods for processing solid nuclear fuels that produce much less radioactive waste than the existing PUREX process.[22]

In 2007, the NAS and the RAS—together with Rosatom, the International Science and Technology Center, and the Geocenter Moscow group—sponsored a workshop on the status of radioactive waste sites that led to preparation of a landmark collection of extended abstracts prepared by more than 60 Russian experts from 20 institutions. They described in detail the status of 15 important radioactive waste sites in Russia that needed greater attention to contain the wastes. Of continuing interest to the international participants were the environmental conditions at or near the Mayak complex described in many abstracts.[23]

In parallel with the focus on upgrading activities at Russian waste sites were two NAS-RAS assessments of the feasibility of establishing an *international* waste site in Russia for receiving and storing international spent nuclear fuel elements from many countries. The first NAS-promoted assessment of this proposal in 2003 addressed the following issues:

- Legal issues, including liability during shipment and reception in Russia of fuel in accordance with international liability conventions.
- Russian legislation for internationally controlled operations.
- Current nuclear power industry trends that would be influenced by a storage facility in Russia.
- Interim storage experience in Asia and Europe.

- A U.S.-Russian agreement on safeguards, physical protection, and U.S. consent rights for some activities, including right of return if requested and separation of plutonium and uranium.[24]

A follow-on assessment in 2005, while expanding on some of the topics discussed in 2003, focused on the following issues:

- Handling of spent nuclear fuel—the international experience.
- Site selection for spent fuel storage and, when appropriate, disposal of high-level waste.
- Establishment of an international storage facility in Russia.
- Utilization of high-level waste.[25]

While the concept of an international spent nuclear fuel storage facility in Russia was realized, the inter-academy reports probably have saved the Russian, U.S., and other governments considerable time and financial expenses in avoiding blind alleys when issues concerning reprocessing, storage, and waste disposal have been raised. Looking to the future, spent nuclear fuel probably will continue to be transported across borders, including the Russian border, for reprocessing, storage, and/or disposal. The presentations included in the reports of the U.S. and Russian academies addressed many important issues that will likely remain of international interest.

STRENGTHENING RADIOLOGICAL SECURITY NOW AND IN THE FUTURE[26]

In 2019, after a pause of a decade in NAS-RAS collaborative efforts to address radiological security, an NAS-RAS workshop on the topic of violent extremism and radiological security was held in Helsinki. This was the first of three workshops on the topic supported primarily by DOE, with additional support provided by the Richard Lounsbery Foundation and the Carnegie Corporation of New York. Upon learning that DOE could not support activities in Russia, at the same time NAS selected Helsinki as the first venue, since for many years the NAS had maintained strong professional relationships with several relevant Finnish institutions.

The second NAS-RAS workshop focusing on radiological security was held in Moscow after DOE decided that such a nongovernmental endeavor in Russia would be important in "keeping the door open for cooperation" while gaining more incisive on-the-ground insights into developments in that country. DOE was awaiting an improvement in the political environment when the department's experts would be able to resume long-standing relationships with Russian government officials that were being only partially maintained through events organized by the IAEA in Vienna. The second workshop also included participation by several European specialists since they had brought important perspectives to the table in Helsinki. As this report was being completed, the NAS was awaiting confirmation from all interested parties that the date of the third workshop in the series—also to be held in Moscow—would soon be confirmed.

There was a significant change in the focus of the new series of three workshops compared with the orientation of the many NAS-RAS events that focused on radiological issues during earlier years. The emphasis during the previous 15 years of collaborative efforts was primarily on developments in Russia—technological capabilities, research and development priorities, and experiences in addressing radiological challenges that had long historical roots during Soviet times. After the pause in cooperation, the workshops discussed in this section address recent developments within both Russia and the United States as well as global trends. The American participants were no longer part-time mentors for Russian colleagues, as the Russians became well aware of many developments abroad concerning the topics on the agendas.

Among the many technical issues on the agendas of the workshops have been the following:

- Reducing insider threats, including security culture among employees; required security facilities and procedures; coping with threats, clandestine storage, and unauthorized transportation of sources; malevolent uses of sources in vulnerable spaces (e.g., shopping malls, sports venues, and transportations terminals).
- Alternative technologies to replace the use of cesium-137 as the radiation source for medical, agricultural, food, industrial, geological, and other purposes; policies, resources, and availability of equipment to support replacement; institutional difficulties in making transitions; and model companies, laboratories, and facilities.
- Permanent disposal of high-level radioactive waste: boreholes and other approaches.
- Improved containers for transportation and storage of low-level radioactive waste.

- Immediate responses to recognized radiological sources at the national and institutional levels, and procedures for accounting for radiological sources of special concern.
- Radiation forensics, including detecting the presence and characteristics of irradiated material.

Among the important information reported during the workshops were presentations on the following activities:

- Russian specialists, in cooperation with international partners, had removed almost 1,000 radioisotope thermoelectric generators from the northern regions of Russia and 4 from Antarctica.
- American institutions had replaced hundreds of cesium-137 sources in hospitals, agricultural centers, and industrial facilities with x-ray (linac) equipment and with other types of approaches.
- The IAEA's database indicated that in 2018, there were 253 incidents in 49 countries of unauthorized use or other inappropriate activities involving nuclear and other radioactive materials.
- As to forensics, there are alternative ways to measure the composition of particles without destroying the samples, ranging from imaging systems to sophisticated mass spectrometry. Alpha track radiography can also be an important tool for sampling of particles in soil and in other material.
- The Lepse floating storage facility near Murmansk had been developed and deployed for operations. Very quickly, the first parcel of nuclear material was sent to Mayak for reprocessing in 2019. International cooperation became important in closing the fuel cycle for use of nuclear energy in the Arctic.
- A plan was developed to create a deep repository for radioactive waste in a granite base in Zheleznogorsk. The plan requires 50 years for implementation while taking into account environmental concerns in the Baikal region.

NOTES

1. NRC (National Research Council). 2007. *U.S.-Russian Collaboration in Combating Radiological Terrorism*. Washington, DC: The National Academies Press, pp. 46–47.

2. Schweitzer, G. E. 2004. *Scientists, Engineers, and Track-Two Diplomacy*. Washington, DC: The National Academies Press, p. 122.

3. NRC. 2019. *The Convergence of Violent Extremism and Radiological Security: Proceedings of a Workshop—in Brief.* Washington, DC: The National Academies Press.

4. NRC. 1999. *Protecting Nuclear Weapons Materials in Russia.* Washington, DC: The National Academies Press, p. 1.

5. Ibid., p. 3.

6. NRC. 2006. *Strengthening Long-Term Nuclear Security: Protecting Weapon-Usable Material in Russia.* Washington, DC: The National Academies Press, p. 2.

7. Op. cit., NRC, 1999, p. 3.

8. Ibid., p. 8.

9. Op. cit., NRC, 2006, p. 57.

10. Op. cit., NRC, 2007, p. 26.

11. Ibid., p. 54.

12. Ibid., pp. 84–85.

13. NRC. 2009. *Cleaning up Sites Contaminated with Radioactive Material: International Workshop Proceedings.* F. Parker, K. Robbins, and G. Schweitzer, eds. Washington, DC: The National Academies Press, p. 162.

14. Ibid., p. 170.

15. Ibid., p. 29.

16. Op. cit., 2007, p. 21.

17. Schweitzer, G. E. 1989. *Techno-Diplomacy: U.S.-Soviet Confrontations in Science and Technology.* New York: Plenum Press, pp. 70, 266.

18. Op. cit., 2007, entire report.

19. Schweitzer, G. E. Conversation with Russian visitors to the United States, 2006.

20. NRC. 2003. *End Points for Spent Nuclear Fuel and High-level Radioactive Waste in Russia and the United States.* Washington, DC: The National Academies Press, p. 4.

21. Glagolenko, Yu. V., Ye. G. Drozhko, and S. I. Rovny. 2009. "Experience in Rehabilitating Contaminated Land and Bodies of Water Around the Mayak Production Association," in *Cleaning Up Sites Contaminated with Radioactive Materials: International Workshop Proceedings.* Washington, DC: The National Academies Press, p. 81.

22. Op. cit., 2003, p. 11.

23. Op. cit., 2007, pp. 26, 50.

24. NRC. 2005. *An International Spent Nuclear Fuel Storage Facility: Exploring a Russian Site as a Prototype: Proceedings of an International Workshop.* Washington, DC: The National Academies Press, pp. ix-xi.

25. NRC. 2008. *Setting the Stage for International Spent Nuclear Fuel Storage Facilities: International Workshop Proceedings.* K. Robbins and G. Schweitzer, eds. Washington, DC: The National Academies Press, pp. ix–x.

26. NRC. 2019. *The Convergence of Violent Extremism and Radiological Security: Proceedings of a Workshop—in Brief.* Washington, DC: The National Academies Press.

27. NRC. 2020. *Scientific Aspects of Violent Extremism, Terrorism, and Radiological Security: Proceedings of a Workshop—in Brief.* Washington, DC: The National Academies Press.

Powerful gamma sources

"PREF"	*"CONS"*
Very hazardous	Difficult to get
Hidden hazard	Problems with transportation
	Easy to disclose

Medium activity gamma sources

"PREF"	*"CONS"*
Hazardous	Problems with transportation
Hidden hazard	Easy to disclose
Easier to get	

Sources based on alpha emitters

"PREF"	*"CONS"*
Can be very hazardous	Usually not large activity
Hidden hazard	
Easy to get	

Radiation sources likely to be attractive to terrorists. "Pref" refers to reasons each source might be preferred by terrorists, and "Cons" refers to reasons a source is less likely to be selected.

Source: Presentation by Mikhail Diordiy on spent radiation sources storage in containers to prevent terrorism and extremism, December 12, 2018.

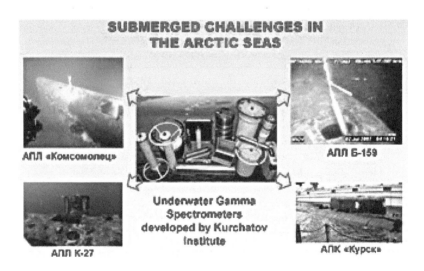

Equipment for monitoring submerged radiological equipment.

Source: Presentation by Oleg Kiknadze, with information from Kurchatov Institute, December 2019.

4

Security of Transportation, Industrial, Construction, Communications, and Other Urban Challenges

Inter-academy security-oriented projects can be useful in stimulating the two governments to focus on specific issues, in setting forth approaches that might seem "out of the box" to governmental officials, and in providing support for policies deemed to be sound. The challenge is not to simply tread ground that has already been thoroughly plowed in inter-governmental consultations. But there should be a reasonable likelihood that non-governmental discussions will help to overcome points of contention.

— NAS report, 2004[1]

The Middle East is a situation that needs to be managed, and terrorism is a struggle, not a war. The most promising areas for U.S.-Russian interactions in combating terrorism are cooperation on the rule of law, emphasis on enforcement of existing treaties, mutual assistance in developing counterterrorism techniques, increased technical exchanges, and continued bilateral and multilateral policy dialogues.

— Paul Bremer, U.S. presidential envoy to Iraq, 2004[2]

Terrorism has become a serious threat characterized by its unpredictable nature, variety of forms, and severe effects on the public. Its organizational structures are losing rigid hierarchy, and they are becoming international networks consisting of practically invulnerable and independently functioning cells. Terrorists are adapting civilian scientific and technological achievements for their criminal activities, with most destructive and deadly impacts.

– Leonid Bolshov, Russian co-chair of
inter-academy workshops, 2004–2008[3]

DEFINING TERRORISM

This chapter is devoted to terrorism, a concept that for decades has rejected attempts to reach global agreement on a clear definition. In 2017, after many pages of recounting the different definitions of terrorism, well-known authority on the history of terrorism Bruce Hoffman settled on the definition set forth in Box 4-1. His commentary leading up to his definition recounted many unsuccessful efforts at the international, national, and local levels to reach a widespread consensus on a relatively brief definition. He consolidated within his definition a variety of generally agreed-upon concepts while omitting other activities that would expand the definition in many directions. Rather than repeating the numerous arguments on whether atrocities committed by military forces, deaths resulting from insurgencies,

---

BOX 4-1
Definition of Terrorism

Terrorism is the deliberate creation and exploitation of fear through violence or the threat of violence in the pursuit of political change. All terrorist acts involve violence or the threat of violence. Also, terrorism is specifically designed to have far-reaching psychological effects beyond the immediate victims of the terrorism attack. It is meant to install fear within, and thereby intimidate, a wider "target audience" that might include a rival ethnic or religious group, an entire country, a national government or political party, or public opinion in general. Terrorism is designed to create power, where there is none, or to consolidate power where there is very little. Through the publicity generated by their violence, terrorists seek to obtain the leverage, influence, and power they otherwise lack to effect political change on either a local or an international scale.
– Bruce Hoffman, 2017, *Inside Terrorism*,
New York: Columbia University Press, p. 44.

---

or simply heinous crimes should be covered by the definition, this report leaves to the judgments of others whether all of the actions included in this chapter and indeed throughout this report should have been called terrorism.

Many activities described in other chapters of this report are clustered as specific manifestations of terrorism, such as biological terrorism and radiological terrorism. Discussions over terminology will continue to be debated. However, the heinous activities set forth below clearly intersect with security concerns at the governmental, institutional, and personal levels.

LAUNCHING OF AN INTER-ACADEMY EFFORT TO IMPROVE INSIGHTS ABOUT TERRORISM

The year 2001 was an unprecedented time for increasing National Academy of Sciences–Russian Academy of Sciences (NAS-RAS) collaborative activities and the bonding of personal and institutional relationships in addressing dangerous global developments. For a number of years, the United States had intensified internal surveillance over groups advocating domestic attacks. The Russian government had put in place a formal interagency organizational framework for counterterrorism led by the Federal Security Service (FSB). These steps helped overcome internal resistance in the two countries for expanding NAS-RAS cooperation in delving deeply into a topic as sensitive as countering terrorism. The first in a series of inter-academy workshops on high-impact terrorism was held in Moscow in June 2001, amidst ominous warning signs indicating the likelihood of more frequent terrorism incidents in both the United States and Russia.

On September 11, 2001 (9/11), a 3-day workshop organized by Russian colleagues with the support of the NAS on the economic challenges confronting nuclear cities in the two countries came to a conclusion in Obninsk, Russia. The radio announcements about the terrorist attacks in the United States suddenly dominated the airwaves, and the celebratory banquet in Obninsk scheduled for that evening was immediately replaced with a very modest solemn supper. Expressions of sympathy and comfort for the American visitors became the order of the days that followed, as most of the Americans struggled to arrange transportation home while their Russian colleagues also worried about their safety from international terrorists in the near future.

By coincidence, the NAS had previously accepted an invitation to participate in another event in Russia immediately following the workshop in Obninsk. This event enabled a representative of the NAS to join leaders from more than 100 Russian universities on a 5-day working cruise on the Volga River. This Russian government–sponsored effort was an important step in developing new pathways for increasing research capabilities at state-supported universities in many Russian cities.

The first overnight stop on the cruise included attendance at an opera in the leading theater in the city of Kazan. As soon as the audience was in place, a 5-minute moment of silence was devoted to the victims of the 9/11 attacks in the United States. Innumerable expressions of personal condolences were then offered throughout the evening. This expression of comradery was repeated at Russian work and leisure venues throughout the duration of the cruise.

The United States experienced highly personal terrorist attacks on a few well-known American political leaders through postal distribution of anthrax-laden letters. Soon, copycat tactics using harmless powder, simulating anthrax, in hundreds of letters followed in Russia. In December 2001, an inter-academy planning meeting was convened in Moscow to chart a course for future cooperation to address the scourge of terrorism. Box 4-2 highlights some of the most significant collaborative activities of the two academies that then followed. They were all intended to improve the capabilities of both Russia and the United States to analyze the rapid spread of terrorism that was of special concern to the governments in the two countries.

Site Visits Associated with NAS-RAS Workshops on Terrorism

Moscow: Ministry of Internal Affairs and its Scientific Institute of Research; EMERCOM's (Ministry for Civil Defense, Emergencies, and Elimination of Consequences of Natural Disasters) Center for Monitoring and Forecasting of Emergency Situations, Research Institute for Civil Defense and Disaster Management, Research Institute for Fire Protection, and Training Facilities; Moscow City Emergency Response Center; Gazprom; Rosenergoatom Crisis Center; Nuclear Safety Research Institute; Bauman Moscow State Technical University; Moscow Engineering and Physics Institute; Alpha Bank; Dubrovka Theater.

St. Petersburg: Northwest Regional Center of EMERCOM; Consolidated Emergency Response Center; City Call-in Center for Emergencies and Disputes; City Public Health Center; Center for Environmental Problems; Institute of Information and Automation; Network of Northwest Coastal Emergency and Rescue Stations along the Gulf of Finland.

BOX 4-2
Inter-Academy Efforts to Improve
Understanding of Terrorism

Important Events
2000: Terrorist attacks in the United States and Russia.

2000: Establishment of an NAS-RAS committee on combating terrorism.

2001: NAS-RAS workshop in Moscow in June on high-Impact terrorism.

2001: 9/11 attack in the United States resulting in about 3,000 deaths.

2001: NAS-RAS planning meeting in December in Moscow focused on terrorism; working groups on energy, transportation, and cyber issues established.

2002: Terrorism incidents at transportation facilities and apartment complexes in Moscow killing several dozen Russian citizens, leading to fatalities of 130 patrons and 50 terrorists during seizure by terrorists of the Dubrovka Theater in Moscow.

2003: NAS-RAS workshop in Moscow on reducing security vulnerabilities and improving resistance to terrorism.

2003: Electrical blackout in New York City during a visit by an RAS team of counterterrorism experts due to collapse of a major power line hundreds of miles away.

2004: The deaths of 360 children, families, and staff and of 50 terrorists during an attack at a school in Beslan in the North Caucasus.

2005: Electrical blackout in Moscow due to a failure at a major power station during an NAS counterterrorism team visit to the center of the city.

2005: NAS-RAS workshop and meetings of three working groups in New York City and Washington, D.C., focused on urban terrorism.

2007: NAS-RAS workshop in Moscow emphasizing biological agents, security of transportation networks, and protection of energy systems.

2009: Celebration in Moscow of the 50th anniversary of NAS-RAS scientific cooperation, including emphasis on continuing cooperation that focused on countering terrorism.

Washington, D.C., area: Washington Metropolitan Area Transit Authority; Department of Homeland Security, Cyber Security Division; Department of Energy East Coast power facilities: Edison Electric Institute; Fairfax County Emergency Services; state of Maryland CHART facility.

New York City and metropolitan area: Office of Emergency Management; Traffic Management Center; Police Department; Fire Department; Port Authority of New York and New Jersey; Polytechnic University; Long Island Electric Power Supply (cause and impact of regional electrical blackout); Con Edison Long Island City headquarters; New Jersey Police Training Commission facilities.

Selected Workshop Presentations

Chapters 2 and 3 of this report highlight issues related to biological and radiological terrorism that were of particular concern during more than two decades of NAS cooperation with Russian partners. Many of these issues were discussed in detail during inter-academy workshops highlighted in those chapters. Others were considered during visits to facilities, primarily in Russia. Still other issues were emphasized in publications prepared by the participants who had participated in the cooperative activities.

Summarized below are comments on various aspects of *other forms* of terrorism that were discussed at four NAS-RAS workshops from 2001 to 2008. Brief summaries of 13 of the more than 75 presentations by workshop participants, including both American and Russian highly respected scientists, are set forth below. They identify many dimensions of terrorism that were considered during that period of intense U.S.-Russian interactions. The primary criteria in selecting the presentations that are cited in this chapter were (a) the influence of the presentation on subsequent collaborative activities of the NAS and the RAS, (b) the relevance at the time of the presentation to major concerns throughout the world, and (c) the lessons learned in dealing with dangerous situations. Details on the presentations as well as commentaries on other aspects of terrorism are included in the four comprehensive reports covering this series of workshops that are identified in the endnotes for this chapter.

Urban Terrorism: A First Perspective

The special features of urban terrorism in Russia, as in other countries, are the abrupt increases in direct damage and particularly the loss of life, the destruction of infrastructure, and indirect negative impacts. These indirect impacts include arousing fear, panic, and paralysis due to the high concentration of bewildered populations, presence of dangerous industrial facilities, and increased opportunities for follow-on destructive activities. One breakdown of targets of terrorists in a variety of urban environments indicated that 85 percent were transportation related (metro systems, buses, train stations, and airports); 5 percent were at markets, theaters, and shops; and only occasionally were urban gas and oil pipelines, power lines, or electrical stations at risk.[4]

Urban Terrorism: A Second Perspective

Urban infrastructures have been the focus of many terrorist acts throughout the world, primarily because they provide the most visible impacts, if not the most casualties. For example, infrastructure interdependencies are extensive. Interruptions in power and communications can close stock exchanges. Electrical power shortages can affect water systems.

The same advances that have enhanced important connectivity can also create new vulnerabilities. Equipment failure can lead to human failure that is then magnified by weather changes and other natural causes. In short, destructive weapons in the hands of terrorists, when linked to disruptions due to innocent errors of others, can be devastating. Thus, highly adaptive, better informed, and more deliberative approaches for reacting to either natural or deliberate disasters are needed.[5]

Access to Explosives

Various methods and procedures for limiting uncontrolled spread of powerful explosives include legislative, organizational, design, and distribution constraints. Serial numbers on cartridges, regular audits of stockpiles, limits on materials used in mining, and more careful handling and sorting of military waste material are important steps when appropriate. The policies of all countries should prevent firms from operating within their borders that do not ensure accountability for industrial destruction devices and dangerous materials that are produced, handled, and/or used.[6]

Firefighting and Rescue

Explosions used in terrorist attacks may partially or completely destroy buildings with associated fires that decrease resistance of structures and thereby cause hazards for firefighters, rescue workers, and the broader population. There may be an urgent need for immediate evacuation of large numbers of people; and panic may quickly follow with fires blocking exit routes, including access to subway stations, bridges, and other escape pathways—thereby leading to mob behavior. Inadequate rescue equipment may also be a problem, with fires erupting in areas covered with wreckage. An essential area of research and development to help mitigate the extent of fire havoc is development of a wide range of robotics technology.[7]

Electromagnetic Terrorism

Sources of powerful electromagnetic pulse-emitting devices or high-voltage pulse generators could be used to disrupt the normal operations of a country's technical systems. Such systems include, for example, airplane takeoff and landing control networks; telecommunications connections; electronic devices controlling nuclear power plant operations; and systems for generation, transmission, and transformation of electrical currents. Also, existing small high-voltage pulse generators make it possible to inject pulses into data transmission chains, housed within a single building, or into electricity supply systems and grounding networks. Such acts could destroy equipment located in many buildings.[8]

Terrorism along Transportation Corridors

A stretch of the New Jersey Turnpike from the Newark Airport to Port Elizabeth has at times been called by terrorism experts "the most dangerous 2 miles in America." The surrounding area has often been used as a staging area by criminals who were planning to cause havoc across the river in New York City. It is not surprising that the state police had long ago adopted the philosophy of combating "all crimes, all hazards, all threats, all the time" with local residents obliged to share responsibility for homeland security. The Regional Operations and Intelligence Center (acting as a "fusion" center) facilitates coordination of information sharing among the many law enforcement agencies in the state. While terrorists plotted their deeds, the police have been on alert preparing themselves to respond to or to recover from man-made and natural disasters should they occur.

Interfacial Vulnerabilities of Transportation Systems

Not all components and interfaces of these systems are given equal attention. In particular, there are no models that realistically incorporate the human components and can then predict the emergency responses of individuals. Transportation systems should be considered as complex, bio-social-machine (*biosoma*) systems with many internal and external connections. The effectiveness of external attempts to disrupt the biosoma systems depends in large measure on resistance and internal coordination of many agencies as well as on the resilience of the systems.

Research is needed to develop approaches that will help assess vulnerability of interfaces. Also, a better understanding of the interactions of human and nonhuman biosoma components of transportation systems would benefit from developments in social network analyses.[9]

Insurgencies and Terrorism

The selection of the areas of activities by terrorist groups can at times be explained by the location of such activities near control centers for insurgency movements that extend from part-time to full-time involvement of disgruntled but well-armed segments of the population. In contrast, foreign or internationally connected networks of fully committed terrorists may be more inclined to seek lightly inhabited areas. When rootless in a given country where combat operations are underway, terrorists may feel unconstrained due to lack of effective support for law enforcement by the populations of the host countries. Often, the psychological and socioeconomic impacts that criminals seek are international, with little regard for the interests of the host country, and as a result, their growing influence and effectiveness can quickly become a dangerous challenge that reaches across borders.[10]

International Dimensions of Cybercrime and Terrorism[11]

Cyberspace has become a locus for banking, finance, and transportation systems, with hundreds of additional applications to follow. At the same time, it attracts malicious activity from vandalism to nation-versus-nation conflict. A suitable framework for international cooperation is essential without delay. An international convention is needed to address the following issues: serious crimes against computer networks, harmonization of national laws, adherence to one or more international conventions by almost all states parties, building stronger international electronic capabilities, support for promoting relevant human rights, forms for enforcement against violators of international conventions, and cost-sharing in implementing international agreements. The realistic issue is not whether to develop an ideal agreement for exchange of insights and know-how, but rather how to have an arrangement that is far better than the current void and can be updated and improved over time.[12]

Future of Terrorism: Tactics and Stealth

Terrorism has often become the tactic of choice for extremist groups and rogue states. It is effective and cheap, and sponsorship may frequently be disguised. Increases in state-sponsored terrorism will be directed primarily against dissidents and critics living abroad. Terrorism is a form of psychological warfare. The response needs to take into account covert actions, deception, black operations, gray and black propaganda, in-depth psychological and motivational studies, and a sound understanding of both national and anti-national factors that influence the decision-making of the terrorist leadership.[13]

Chemical Threats and Responses

Four examples of important types of chemical terrorism are as follows: (1) release of a military-grade chemical warfare agent against a civilian target, (2) sabotage of a chemical manufacturing plant or storage facility (including a rail tank car) where toxic chemicals are held in gaseous or liquid form, (3) contamination of public water facilities or food supplies with toxic agents, and (4) targeted use of chemical agents to assassinate specific individuals.

Priority should be given to preventing the most likely types. Of course, many other types of incidents, such as release of a military-grade chemical, should not be neglected. Priority should be given to training hazmat teams, organizing medical triage units, and expanding capability for treatment of large numbers of victims. Additional federal hotlines, drug stockpiles, and rapid response teams are frequently needed.[14]

Security of Natural Gas and Oil Pipelines

Improvement of pipeline security depends in large measure on better equipment and technology for new pipeline construction, more reliable diagnostics, and modern methods for rapidly eliminating the consequences of accidents. Also of importance are development of effective measures and equipment for preventing attacks against elements of the oil and gas infrastructure. No matter what new equipment or capability may be proposed, it will probably increase the cost of a barrel of oil. As long as oil and natural gas are a foundation on which the world economy functions, protection of access to oil and gas will retain high priority regardless of increases in the price of a barrel of oil.[15]

Technological Terrorism

This type of terrorism has often been defined as destructive actions directed against infrastructure elements that are critically important for national security. The primary impact factors of such actions are significantly higher (tens or hundreds of times higher) than less dangerous activities that affect only a small portion of the public and the surrounding environment. The impact factors are based in large measure on the levels of dynamism, selection of the timing, capability of terrorists to choose destructive attack scenarios, public perception of the terrorism risk, complexity of the types of threats, and the capability of the terrorists to self-learn from each attempt. In specific scenarios, terrorists may be interested solely in initial impacts, while officials of the facility under assault may have much greater concerns over the secondary and lasting impacts.[16]

Events and Site Visits of Special Interest

From 2001 to 2009, terrorism-related special briefings, site visits, and other activities that were linked to the workshops were of special interest to NAS and RAS specialists. Several of these activities are described below.

Terrorism in a Moscow Theater

Following the terrorist occupation of the Dubrovka Theater in Moscow in 2002, many questions arose in the press and during public and private discussions of governmental officials about details of the rescue of hundreds of entrapped spectators in the theater, the deaths of 130 spectators, and the killing of 50 terrorists. Issues of particular concern included inadequate coordination of rescue activities of many government agencies, chaotic conditions in the parking lot of the theater due to excessive use of cell phones that complicated rescue efforts, and use of a pharmaceutical spray that stunned the terrorists inside the theater—along with many spectators—as the rescue teams entered the theater. At the request of the NAS, the RAS arranged for a representative of the Russian government to provide an account of the rescue activities and respond to questions during an NAS-RAS workshop. This account was the most detailed report by the government (the FSB) that was made available to the public at that time. A summary of the presentation is included in Appendix C of this report, and the complete presentation is included in the proceedings of the 2003 workshop published by the NAS.[17]

Terrorism at a School in the North Caucasus

Another public-relations challenge occurred following the killing by Chechen terrorists of 360 adults and students at a school in Beslan in the North Caucasus in 2003. During the aftermath, confusion abounded about the details of the fiery confrontation between the terrorists and the military forces working with the local police, and why it was not stopped before it began. The battle ended in the deaths of hundreds of children in an unprecedented bloodbath in modern Russia. For months, acrimonious charges were leveled at the authorities at the local, regional, and national levels for allowing such an event to take place. Once again, at the request of the NAS, the RAS arranged for a government spokesperson to provide the first publicly released detailed report by the government (the FSB) describing in detail the activities at Beslan, the government's view on the causes for the incident, and then commentary on the appropriateness of the response. A summary of the presentation is included in Appendix D, and the complete presentation is included in the proceedings of an inter-academy workshop in 2004.[18]

Coping with Suicide Bombers

In 2005, the NAS and the RAS held a workshop on urban terrorism in Moscow. The NAS invited the New York City Police Department to send a representative to the workshop to discuss the challenges confronting police departments in large cities during the age of terrorism. The department selected a senior specialist who was on temporary duty in Tel Aviv, working with Israeli colleagues in strengthening local approaches for countering terrorism. This specialist captivated the audience in Moscow with his description of the steps that were being taken in Israel to prevent incidents involving suicide bombers, who had been wreaking havoc in Israeli cities. His additional comments on his day-to-day duties—first, in the most impoverished areas of New York City, and then in Tel Aviv—provided a dramatic wake-up call for the attendees to take extreme measures for countering drastic criminal approaches such as suicide bombing. Afterward, the questions and comments on his presentation were endless.[19]

Power Outages in New York and Moscow

Reliable electrical power was a common theme during inter-academy discussions of terrorist activities in urban areas. While some workshop presentations addressed this topic, specialists from both countries had unexpected opportunities to become personally involved. In August 2003, several members of the core group of Russian scientists responsible for arranging inter-academy workshops were in New York when the power in the city failed. Staying in a hotel late into the evening with no electricity was not a pleasant experience. Then in May 2005, during discussions in Moscow about urban terrorism, an NAS group of specialists and staff had considerable difficulty traveling from the center of Moscow to a hotel several miles away when the electrical power throughout a large segment of Moscow failed. After a 3-hour struggle through large crowds, the team finally made its way to the hotel. The blackout lasted for 3 more hours until the flow of electricity was finally restored.

Training Facilities in Moscow and New Jersey

Following the terrorism incident at the Dubrovka Theater, the Russian national emergency response organization EMERCOM on two occasions invited American specialists interested in the practical aspects of countering terrorism in the field to visit its extensive training facilities in Moscow. The first visit shortly after the Dubrovka incident in 2002 focused largely on additions made to the training courses offered to EMERCOM personnel. Up-to-date communication equipment was on display. A specific concern at the Dubrovka Theater had been the overloading of hundreds of cell phones that belonged to responders, relatives of hostages, and the general public that congregated in the parking lot. Several improvements were promptly made. New emergency channels were to be used only by personnel from EMERCOM and other government agencies with relevant responsibilities. More modern cell phones had been purchased as technology rapidly advanced. Finally, a new mobile control center was fully equipped and was ready for deployment.

Meanwhile, the New Jersey State Police had become a strong supporter for exchanges of experience with Russian counterparts through the NAS program. The police invited Russian counterparts to visit the New Jersey Police Training Commission facilities, which dates back many decades, and to observe training programs. This direct contact continued beyond involvement of NAS as a facilitator.

Terrorism Response Centers in Moscow and New York

Closely linked to workshop discussions on countering urban terrorism were visits by both Russian and American workshop participants to the New York City Office of Emergency Management and the Moscow Crisis Situation Management Center. The New York center was dramatically upgraded following the 9/11 attacks to accommodate up to 100 specialists from a wide variety of organizations with headquarters in the city. The Moscow center also brought together a variety of organizations responsible for many security aspects confronting the population of the city. As a follow-up to workshop discussions on the reduction of risk in metropolitan centers, NAS representatives were invited to attend two workshops in Moscow organized by the center. These workshops delved in greater detail into preparedness to prevent terrorist attacks in the city. A considerable emphasis was placed on the problem of fires, with more than 7,000 fires in Moscow during 2002 that required emergency responses by the city's firefighters.

Emergency Response Facilities in Northwest Russia

Following an inter-academy workshop in 2003 in Moscow, the American participants had the opportunity to visit three emergency response facilities in St. Petersburg and along the coast of the Gulf of Finland.

St. Petersburg's Interagency Council for Response to Emergencies had just held its first meeting in a spacious and very functional center. Electronic zoom maps of the details of the city were frequently displayed. More than 20 organizations participated in addressing any indications of terrorist attacks or other criminal activities in the city. The impressive agenda for the first meeting emphasized the importance of leadership responsibilities for various areas of activities.

A second facility was the Emergency Response Center, which received all emergency telephone calls. In many respects, it was an expanded version of an upgraded 9/11 call center in the United States. According to the staff, many calls related to family disputes. With extensive patience, considerable effort was taken to resolve each problem by telephone. A well-qualified psychologist was always on duty and usually took the lead in responding to calls that involved family disputes or other types of mental disturbances. The psychologists were patient and effective, and they were always in high demand.

The final stop was the headquarters for the EMERCOM rescue teams that patrolled coastal openings to the sea and did not hesitate to use speed boats when necessary. They divided their time between (a) responding to calls for help due to transportation difficulties or concerns over personal safety and (b) investigating reports of criminal activity in the barren lands of the north. When necessary, they could ask the maritime service, the navy, or aircraft patrols for assistance.

AFTERTHOUGHTS

This chapter has discussed inter-academy cooperation in addressing different types of terrorism during both times of political rapprochement between the two countries and times of strains in the political relationship. During the early years of cooperation, the governments of the two countries were uncertain as to the effectiveness of their own approaches in dealing with threats from abroad, and at times from turmoil within their own borders. In both Washington and Moscow there frequently was considerable skepticism that U.S.-Russian joint efforts could be effective. It soon became clear that security-oriented projects were most likely to receive attention if the governments of the two countries had been involved in making available relevant unclassified information and in facilitating access to government experts who were also working on the issues addressed by the academies. But even under the best of circumstances, academy efforts could have only limited *near-term* impact given the large U.S. and Russian governmental endeavors being devoted to a broad range of security issues.

At the same time, academy projects were useful in stimulating the governments to act on important issues by suggesting approaches that might have seemed "out of the box" but nevertheless offered the possibility of success to government officials. In addition, suggestions for modest modifications of government policies that had not been particularly effective were on occasion welcomed. One measure of success of inter-academy cooperation was the effect of nongovernmental discussions and related activities on opening new governmental avenues for cooperation while avoiding or overcoming points of contention.

In the longer term, inter-academy efforts can make a significant difference by documenting conclusions and recommendations in publicly available reports. At times, these reports can provide a basis for both government officials and the public to debate issues in a more informed manner that might otherwise be possible. Also, when government officials who have been interested in academy issues change assignments, the reports can be helpful in the education of their successors.

That said, an overriding consideration is in order. In other words, "successful" cooperation should not be measured simply by the number of topics that are addressed. Rather, the likelihood of serious governmental consideration of findings and the quality of the supporting reports that are generated are the most important indicators of success.[20]

NOTES

All of the notes except notes 1 and 11 cite presentations by individual specialists at workshops on the indicated topics.

1. Schweitzer, G. E. 2004. *Scientists, Engineers, and Track-Two Diplomacy.* Washington, DC: The National Academies Press, p. 61.
2. Bremer, L. P. 2002. "International and Domestic Terrorism," in *High-Impact Terrorism: Proceedings of a Russian-American Workshop.* Washington, DC: The National Academies Press, p. 53.
3. Bolshov, L., R. Arutyunyan, E. Melikhova, and O. Pavlovsky. 2006. "Unauthorized Use of Radiation Sources: Measures to Prevent Attacks and Mitigate Consequences," in *Countering Urban Terrorism in Russia and the United States: Proceedings of a Workshop.* Washington, DC: The National Academies Press, p. 133.
4. Frolov, K. 2006. "Problems of Urban Terrorism in Russia," in *Countering Urban Terrorism,* p. 35.
5. Tien, J. 2006. "A Decision Informatics Approach to Urban Emergency Management," in *Countering Urban Terrorism,* p. 79.
6. Matseevich, B. 2002. "Selected Technologies and Procedures Intended to Restrict Unauthorized Access to Explosives," in *High-Impact Terrorism,* p. 168.
7. Kopylov, N. 2006. "Special Characteristics of Firefighting in Urban Areas," in *Countering Urban Terrorism,* p. 60.
8. Fortov, V., and Y. V. Parfyonov. 2009. "Electromagnetic Terrorism: Threat to the Security of the State Infrastructure," in *Countering Terrorism: Biological Agents, Transportation Networks, and Energy Systems: Summary of a U.S.-Russian Workshop.* Washington, DC: The National Academies Press, p. 186.

9. Bugliarello, G. 2009. "A Note on the Interfacial Vulnerabilities of Transportation Systems," in *Countering Terrorism*, p. 95.

10. Adams, R. 2006. "Does the Emergence of Insurgencies Provide for Terrorism?" in *Countering Urban Terrorism*, p. 130.

11. After a year of inter-academy discussions (2003–2004) about the importance of improving cyber security in both countries, neither academy was able to gain permission from governmental security authorities to discuss technical approaches. Therefore, inter-academy discussions in this area were limited to opportunities for international cooperation on and approaches to university-level education in computer technology.

12. Goodman, S. 2002. "Preventing and Responding to Cybercrime and Terrorism: Some International Dimensions," in *High-Impact Terrorism*, p. 198.

13. Probst, P. 2002. "Terrorism Future: Tactics, Strategy, and Stealth," in *High-Impact Terrorism,* p. 260.

14. Tucker, J. 2002. "Chemical Terrorism, Assessing Threats and Responses," in *High-Impact Terrorism*, p. 117.

15. Serebryakov, S. G. 2009. "The Problem of Oil and Natural Gas Pipeline Security," in *Countering Terrorism*, p. 189.

16. Makhutov, N. 2009. "Characteristics of Technological Terrorism. Scenarios and Impact Factors," in *Countering Terrorism*, p. 53.

17. Kolesnikov, Y. 2009. "Lessons Learned from the *Nord-Ost* Terrorist Attack in Moscow from the Standpoint of Russian Security and Law Enforcement Agencies," in *Russian Views on Countering Terrorism during Eight Years of Dialogue: Extracts from Proceedings of Four U.S.-Russian Workshops*. Washington, DC: The National Academies Press, p. 93.

18. Kovalenko, G. 2006. "On the Events in Beslan," in *Countering Urban Terrorism*, p. 167.

19. Dzikansky, M. 2009. "The Phenomenon of Suicide Bombings in Israel: Lessons Learned," in *Countering Terrorism*, p. 189.

Strasbourg, France – November 14, 2015: French Police checking vehicles on the 'Bridge of Europe' between Strasbourg and Kehl, Germany, as a security measure in the wake of attacks in Paris.
Photo credit: Adrian Hancu.

Destruction in Mosul, Iraq in 2019.
Source: Presentation by Scott Atran on violent extremism and sacred values. Photograph provided by the NAS.

5

Interests in the Middle East and Beyond

The main front against international terrorism is no longer in Afghanistan, where the United States is losing momentum. A fair solution to the Palestinian issue beyond a roadmap, and with a true Palestinian-Israeli compromise, is necessary. As to the Middle East Quartet, its mission must be broader. Participants should include participation of regional leaders and also China and India.
— Former Prime Minister Yevgeny Primakov, during an NAS-RAS dialogue in Moscow, 2009.

Jihadists are probably fewer than 100,000 in number, with annual budgets totaling less than $10 million. Western governments have spent hundreds of millions of dollars, if not more, in combating jihadists, and it is difficult to identify our successes. What are we doing wrong?
— Comment at a workshop in Paris organized by the NAS, RAS, and French National Center for Scientific Research, 2017

International attention is focusing on steps that were promptly taken by Prime Minister Jacinda Ardern to limit access to dangerous weapons in New Zealand following the attack on Al Noor Mosque in Christchurch in 2019. These steps have set a positive tone for bringing together policy makers, scientists, and the general public at home and abroad.
— Joint statement of participants in the NAS-RAS workshop in Abu Dhabi 2 weeks after the attack, 2019

POLITICAL AND SECURITY CONTEXT

As highlighted in previous chapters, the National Academy of Sciences (NAS) cooperated extensively during the early 2000s with its partners in Russia, primarily the Russian Academy of Sciences (RAS), and with government agencies and foundations in the United States in supporting, analyzing, and implementing programs and projects clarifying the spread of violence and terrorism. By the end of the first decade, the Russian government and many analytical and research institutions in Moscow recognized the importance of sustained collaboration involving Russia and the United States in addressing a wide range of global problems, including security issues. In Washington, the Department of State and the leadership of the NAS also considered that continuing exchange of views on security-related issues was important.

At the same time, the leaders of Russia seemed determined to rely less than in years past on analytical approaches that were driven in significant measure by Western visions of the future. These leaders were committed to promoting Russia's aspirations. They were prepared to work with other governments, including the U.S. government when appropriate, while being very active in developing the contours of the global future in many forums.

Outside the borders of Russia, the other successor states of the former Soviet Union had become arenas for conflicting U.S. and Russian interests and actions affecting both internal and external policies and programs of some of these states. U.S.-Russian collaboration in dealing with challenges confronting the governments of these states had become difficult. At the same time, the future of several nations in the Middle East beyond the boundaries of the former Soviet Union was of increasing concern to both governments. The contribution of informal dialogue to improve understanding of developments in the Middle East and beyond is addressed in this chapter.

In 2009, President Barack Obama announced new engagement of the United States in promoting peace in the Middle East during a speech in Washington as the Arab Spring began to emerge, initially in Tunisia and Egypt and then spreading to other countries. He announced that the United States would establish a new fund for support of technological development in Muslim-majority countries that would help transfer ideas in the laboratories to products in the marketplace and thereby create more jobs. New centers of scientific excellence would be supported in Africa, the Middle East, and Southeast Asia. New American science envoys would stimulate programs to help develop more reliable sources of energy, create green jobs, digitize records, provide clean water, and grow new crops. These promises raised considerable attention within U.S. science-oriented institutions, including the NAS.[1]

Meanwhile in Moscow, former Prime Minister Yevgeny Primakov had retired from his governmental position and had become a leading scholar within one of the well-respected RAS institutes. He and his team focused considerable attention on the future of the Middle East, an area that had been at the top of his personal interests for decades. At the same time, Thomas Pickering, a former undersecretary of state with considerable experience in the Middle East, had become an active NAS interlocutor of nongovernmental meetings on many topics of interest to Russia. Thus, it was not surprising that the RAS quickly accepted an NAS proposal to initiate an inter-academy dialogue on common interests in the Middle East led by Primakov and Pickering, including concern over acts of terrorism in the region. The general view of leaders of both academies seemed to be the following: Perhaps the academies of the two countries could help assess old and new approaches to reduce growing animosities within and between countries located in the Middle East.

Box 5-1 lists the series of NAS-RAS activities during the past decade related to this recognition of mutual interests in some of the security issues in the Middle East, and at times spreading out beyond the Middle East. It includes dialogues focused on the Middle East led by Primakov and Pickering. Then it concludes with views on violence and security in a wider variety of countries expressed at a series of NAS-RAS workshops in several countries.

INTER-ACADEMY DIALOGUES UNDER CO-CHAIRMANSHIP OF FORMER PRIME MINISTER YEVGENY PRIMAKOV AND FORMER UNDERSECRETARY OF STATE THOMAS PICKERING[2]

Three bilateral dialogues, each extended over 3 days, involved a total of 50 participants selected by the NAS and the RAS. During each dialogue, about 15 participants presented their observations on developments in various countries/regions in the greater Middle East extending from North Africa to Afghanistan. Discussions by participants about the themes of the individual presentations followed. An important objective of each dialogue was to create a foundation for follow-up communications between American and Russian analysts with common interests. The participants also kept the two governments apprised of commonalities and differences among nongovernmental colleagues in viewing the situation in the Middle East from different vantage points.

BOX 5-1
Important Events Related to Inter-Academy Cooperation

2009: Establishment by Presidents Obama and Medvedev of the Commission on Bilateral Cooperation, including cooperation on terrorism.

2009: First Primakov-Pickering inter-academy dialogue in Moscow. A broad scan of many developments across the Middle East.

2011: Second Primakov-Pickering dialogue in Washington, D.C. Likely impacts of the emerging Arab Spring together with additional overviews of developments throughout the Middle East.

2011: Third Primakov-Pickering dialogue in Moscow. Emphasis on Israeli-Palestinian relations, with working groups that addressed water and health challenges. Then there was a broad scan of developments from throughout the region with particular attention to developments in Afghanistan, Iran, and Iraq.

2014–2015: NAS-initiated consultations in Moscow by American scientists to explore the continuance of interest in inter-academy discussions that could improve understanding of ethnic violence and of terrorism in the Middle East and adjacent areas.

2016: NAS-RAS workshop in Moscow on extremism and terrorism, with visits to the Institute of World Economy and International Relations, Institute of Europe, Institute of Oriental Studies, Institute of Ethnology and Anthropology, and Memorial Human Rights Center.

2017: NAS-RAS workshop in Paris with reports on field research and analyses of the roots and trajectories of violent extremism in Europe and the Middle East and a visit to the French National Center for Scientific Research.

2018: NAS-RAS workshop in Helsinki on violent extremism and radiological security. Related staff visit to Chernobyl (see also Chapter 3).

2019: NAS-RAS workshop in Abu Dhabi on violent extremism in the Middle East and beyond.

2019: NAS-RAS workshop in Moscow on the scientific aspects of violent extremism and radiological security. Visit by American workshop participants to RADON in Sergiev Posad, near Moscow (see also Chapter 3).

2022: NAS-RAS workshop in Moscow on violent extremism and innovative approaches to strengthen radiological security (planned for late fall 2021).

During each dialogue, representatives of the Russian and U.S. governments provided comments about the interests and concerns of their governments with the expectation of feedback from the participants that would be of particular interest.

At the outset, participants agreed that there would not be formal reports on the content of the dialogues, but at the same time the NAS and the RAS could provide interested parties on the content of the discussions. Indeed, they considered informing others of the content of the dialogues a good idea, since the concept of the dialogues was to encourage future discussions of both old and new ideas to reduce uncertainties about the reasons for hostilities. Therefore, a few comments during each of the dialogues, based on informal notes prepared by the NAS participants and staff, are summarized below.

Dialogue 1 – December 2009, Moscow

John Beyrle, U S. ambassador to Russia, underscored the importance of cooperation in dealing with problems of mutual interest, emphasizing the need for patience and perseverance in addressing a wide range of issues throughout the Middle East. He reported that the U.S. president was seeking a comprehensive regional solution to the area's many problems, including the conflicting aspirations of Israel, Syria, and Lebanon. The ambassador welcomed Israel's 10-month moratorium on settlements. He emphasized that stabilization of Afghanistan and resolution of the Arab-Israeli conflict are clearly among the most vexing problems facing the world. The ambassador expressed appreciation for Russian support for the international coalition in Afghanistan (e.g., facilitation of international cargoes and prevention of narcotics trafficking). He concluded with a call for coordination between the two governments, noting the importance of transparency during unofficial but important U.S.-Russian discussions of policy adjustments as problems continued to arise in these and additional areas of concern.

Yevgeni Primakov, former prime minister of Russia, underscored that the Israeli cabinet clearly planned to maintain the political status quo while continuing to build settlements on the West Bank and in East Jerusalem. He observed that President Obama apparently abandoned his initial search for peace due to political pressure at home. Regarding the policy of the Palestinians, a schism within the movement crippled their negotiating position. A possible approach to move forward would be to expand the Middle East Quartet to include China and India, to exchange small pieces of territory that would reduce travel limitations, and to establish East Jerusalem as a partition of the city of Jerusalem. Finally, he urged that the concept of the right of return should be accepted; but the difficulties in implementing the concept should be recognized by all and should not prevent consideration of new opportunities for progress in resolving other issues.

Thomas Pickering, former U.S. ambassador to Russia and to Israel and then undersecretary of state, focused on ending U.S. military engagement in Iraq and Afghanistan, promoting peace and stability in Pakistan, and diffusing advanced weaponry throughout the Middle East, including the access by radicals to powerful weapons. He suggested that suppression of increased violence throughout the region might result from a coordinated U.S.-Russian response. Regarding Iraq, the primary concern was that after a U.S. exodus from Iran, rule by the majority, minority rights, and fair distribution of oil earnings would be maintained and not displaced by a civil war. As to Pakistan, it was not difficult to imagine disintegration of the country as well as the potential use of nuclear weapons in confrontations with India. Finally, it was clear that in discussing approaches of the United States and Russia in Afghanistan and in Pakistan, the interests of the two Asian-oriented countries must be considered as interwoven.

Alexei Vasiliev, director of the Institute for African Studies in Moscow, commented on the "tsunami" of Arab revolutions. Focusing on the northern tier of African states, he underscored that revolutions had spread to these countries not because of their extreme poverty, nor had they spread because of hunger or economic stagnation. They had spread because of the actions of Egypt's and Tunisia's regimes that were among the most tyrannical and oppressive in the world. The youth bulge was also a significant aspect of the crisis, with a surge in youth unemployment having a particularly destabilizing effect. The young people soon possessed a new powerful tool of organizations and leadership (without leaders), namely information technology. Libyan Colonel Muammar Gadafi's regime had enough of a social base to survive without confronting the military might of NATO. The masses were able to use internet technology in many ways in these and other developing countries, as well as in developed countries.

These four keynote presentations were then followed by many hours of comments by the presenters and others on a wide variety of issues of considerable importance to the two governments. Throughout the workshop, issues were addressed from different directions. Almost all interventions recognized that while the two governments may disagree on the roots and resolutions of animosities that plagued the region, the United States and Russia had common interests in reducing the armed conflicts that are underway in the region or were on the horizon.

Dialogue 2 – February 2011, Washington, D.C.

Dialogue 2 was held in the wake of a U.S.-Russian nongovernmental conference in Malta 1 month earlier that had considered some of the topics on this dialogue's agenda.

Several of the conclusions of the Malta conference, which were also highlighted by the participants during the dialogue, included the following:

- Since the bilateral track between Israel and the Palestinians had been blocked, it was time to relaunch more multilateral negotiations, bringing in regional actors such as Turkey and Iran. An international conference in Moscow could run parallel to the intergovernmental proximity talks, which the U.S. envoy George Mitchell was promoting with the Israelis and the Palestinians.
- A less ambitious idea was to hold an urgent meeting of the Middle East Quartet to develop specific proposals for a resolution of the conflict with a time line for implementation. China and India should be included.
- Another urgent need was to develop practical ideas for creation of a Middle East security system, which would not only provide security for Israel but also build a regional security system for all.

Against this background and other recent developments, the dialogue continued with discussions of three overriding regional concerns: ensuring a peaceful transition in Egypt, preventing coups in Jordan and Syria, and avoiding the worsening of the situation in Lebanon. The discussion then turned to the Israeli-Palestinian situation and to documents released by Al Jazeera that indicated the closeness of reaching an Israeli-Palestinian agreement under Israel's Ehud Olmert government.

After extended conversations about the Israeli-Palestinian challenges, attention focused on Egypt, including common U.S.-Russian concerns such as spread of terrorism, development of weapons of mass destruction, changes in the price of energy resources, and Islamist extremism. Discussion also focused on whether interventions by moderate Islamists such as those in Turkey should be tolerated. There was considerable concern about economic issues that fomented turmoil in Egypt. Many of the participants urged that economic recovery be considered paramount. However, there was considerable disagreement as to whether "color revolutions" were an appropriate analogy for events in Egypt.

The participants discussed many other issues throughout the Middle East, including poverty and frustration among the people. They focused on practical issues that could improve the lives of the people, starting with health and water issues. They explored many practical measures that could be taken by governments and nongovernmental organizations to start improvement in relations between hostile groups on the ground from a technical perspective.

Several participants underscored that there were political challenges in every area, but most were convinced that animosities could be reduced to clarify the benefit of all. The participants welcomed the suggestion that the U.S. and Russian academies consider on-the-ground actions they could take for health and water issues, which were to be discussed in more detail at the next dialogue.

The concluding session focused on developments in Iran. The Russian experts suggested that a joint effort on Afghanistan might be an approach to engage the Iranians. They noted that Iran was embargoing oil being sent to Afghanistan to complicate shipments of U.S. military supplies to the region. At the same time, illegal immigration into Iran from Afghanistan was increasing, while Russian relations with Afghanistan were improving.

According to the Russian experts, a regional security system could include Iran. They then posed a question as to whether the United States could join with Russia in providing security for nuclear facilities that the Iranians were constructing. The American participants responded that they were very concerned about the safety of these facilities, but the United States had difficulties in engaging Iran.

The American participants noted that Israel was also very concerned about any type of attack on Iran, and the United States was cooperating with Israel in developing a missile shield. Several American discussants underscored the need for Iranian transparency. A Russian participant responded that the Iranians would be more cooperative if no one was threatening them.

In conclusion, the participants discussed the topics for engaging the Iranians in addressing developments in the Caspian Sea—fishing, pollution, oil development, and environmental conservation, for example. An American expert noted that perhaps future discussions could involve representatives of all of the littoral states of the Caspian Sea.

Dialogue 3 – November 2011, Moscow

This dialogue focused primarily on the Arab Spring, the Israel-Palestine confrontation as a continuing major concern, developments in Syria, and the importance of addressing regional health and water issues. Regarding the Arab Spring, the following ramifications were among the many that were highlighted in the discussions:

- Protest movements and the demise of regimes occurring in several countries in the Arab East created prerequisites for political approaches to be redefined.
- Arab economic policies were reactive in nature and prevented ruling elites from taking any types of peaceful measures that were urgently required.
- Social rebellions led to the reduction of economic performance, wage arrears, and disruption of internal economic relations.
- An on-rushing financial crisis throughout the region created long-term economic destabilization.
- It was not possible to foresee any changes in modification of the economic or social structures of Arab countries.
- The new elite throughout the region may draw lessons from the past and even go as far as adopting more complicated low-budget, monetary schemes implemented through the use of force.

Turning to the perpetual crisis in Israel, Russian experts presented their views on the following developments:

- The Palestine Liberation Organization (PLO) had promoted a reconciliation with Hamas and international recognition of the PLO as substitutes for the negotiation process.
- Israel had imposed its own precondition for negotiations—acceptance of Israel as a Jewish state. This clearly reflected an Israeli lack of interest in peace negotiations that might lead to defining the border or dealing with Jerusalem.
- The Middle East Quartet had been unable to reach agreement on anything more substantive than a call for multilateral talks.
- In response to dynamic developments throughout the region, Israel would probably turn to a buildup of self-reliance forces and military solutions to problems.

The dialogue then turned to a focus on Israel-Turkey negotiations, beginning with resumption of peace talks, which were portrayed as an indirect path toward peace that had been established. However, this effort came to a close with the start of the Israeli offensive in Gaza, which destroyed an industrial zone that was under construction with Turkish support. It seemed clear that Turkey could no longer keep a neutral position that was essential for a moderator. This development also affected the prospect of future Israeli-Syrian negotiations by erecting additional hurdles in the way of Turkey returning to negotiations involving Syria.

Focusing on the West Bank, the Russian team did not include a medical specialist in the delegation, despite a commitment to discuss collaboration on mutual health interests on the West Bank. An American expert reported on the success of the activities of the Rostropovich-Vishnevskaya Foundation in providing the financial resources and medical skills for a child-vaccination program involving tens of thousands of children on the West Bank. At the same time, the experts who led that program quickly challenged the priority being given by Palestinian scientists to their attempt to develop advanced health medications in competition with Western pharmaceutical companies. These experts had urged that available resources for improving health on the West Bank be given to reducing common diseases that could be handled by well-trained nurses who were in short supply.

Finally, regarding the shortage and appropriation of locally available water, the participants in the dialogue quickly agreed that water issues should be handled on a track separate from other aspects of Israeli-Palestinian negotiations. If water is not considered as a separate issue, disagreements over water sharing will block meaningful negotiations on almost all other issues.

An abbreviated summary of the important discussion about water availability and allocation during the dialogue is as follows. It was unlikely that the Israelis and Palestinians would be able to reach a permanent status water agreement if their negotiations focused only on the issues of water rights and allocation of the natural water resources of the Jordan River basin. In the past, Israeli, Jordanian, and Palestinian negotiators had discussed the need to consider working together—and with the international donor community—to develop additional water resources. Seawater desalination had been the main technology discussed in many forums for generating additional fresh water. Improvements to existing water infrastructure and implementation of improved water management policies would help make use of existing resources more equitable. The construction of new infrastructure, especially for the Palestinians, would be needed to make best use of any additional fresh water that might become available. But the water availability and allocation issues have defied and will probably continue to defy resolution for decades.

THE ROOTS AND TRAJECTORIES OF VIOLENT EXTREMISM

This segment of the chapter presents a few of the highlights of five workshops on violent extremism carried out under the auspices of the NAS and the RAS from 2016 to 2019. The first workshop in 2016 was primarily an exploratory workshop in Moscow that set the stage for activities that would follow. The Russian organizer published a few of the highlights of the exploratory workshop. They included presentations about foreign fighters traveling from Dagestan to the Middle East, activities of the Taliban in Afghanistan, the historical context for the emergence of ISIS, ways to counter extremism and radicalization, recent developments in Iraq and Syria, and open source data for tracing worldwide terrorism patterns.[3] More expansive reports (proceedings-in-brief) for the other four workshops were distributed and posted on the NAS website.[4]

Each of the workshops addressed on-the-ground developments in areas in turmoil while considering research and analytical efforts based on reports about on-the-ground challenges being faced by researchers in many countries. On the first day of the second workshop in Paris in 2017, terrorists using explosive devices disrupted activities on the Champs-Élysées, thus adding a sense of urgency to the inter-academy deliberations in Paris that began 2 hours after the explosion. Following the fourth workshop in Abu Dhabi, a Russian participant immediately traveled to the United Arab Emirates border with Yemen in response to a request by his government to address violence in the region, again highlighting the relevance of the workshop discussions to current events. A sixth NAS-RAS workshop has been postponed from 2020 to 2022 due to the COVID-19 pandemic.

Rather than reviewing the presentations and findings for each workshop, this summary consolidates discussion points of particular interest throughout the workshops under several headings. Workshops 4 and 5 were on the general topic of violent extremism and radiological security. The science and technological aspects of radiological security are summarized in Chapter 3, which is devoted to radiological terrorism. The discussion in this chapter highlights the commentaries about violence and extremism presented at the workshops, but it does not address technical aspects of radiological terrorism, which were considered in Chapter 3.

All of the workshops were designed to bring to the table a variety of perspectives on violent extremism—in its formative stages, its manifestations, and responses by the affected locales, governments, and populations to recent incidents and perceived future threats. Activities before, during, and after incidents in a variety of countries were considered—with particular emphasis on developments within Muslim-majority countries. While government officials of the countries where the workshops were held were well informed about many aspects of the deliberations, they were not asked to provide governmental perspectives on the topics under discussion.

As noted, some of the presentations were based on personal observations of participants who had carried out research or conducted assessments in strife-torn areas, particularly in the Middle East but also to a limited extent in North Africa and Europe. Of special interest were personal observations by workshop participants who had engaged in research and related activities in Spain, Morocco, Tunisia, Iraq, Syria, and Dagestan. Also, the workshop discussions recognized the changing political landscapes throughout the entire Arab world. An important emphasis was on new and evolving approaches to cause havoc. The enhanced capabilities of the international community to articulate the threats and to detect and resist these threats were also highlighted. For example, access to the internet had both helped and hindered terrorist operations, while recruitment of technologically oriented scientists and engineers to join jihad movements posed new types of concerns.[5]

A few examples of other views expressed during the workshops are as follows:

Overarching Challenges:

- There are profound differences between conflict and terrorism. Such differences exist in (a) describing the political, economic, and social frameworks before, during, and after violence; (b) addressing rehabilitation and reconstruction; (c) considering technical and/ or financial assistance to be provided by governments or local communities to resist or respond to attacks; and (d) recognizing shortcomings of existing institutions in understanding current trends concerning the causes and long-term impacts of terrorism.
- Managers, researchers, and teachers are not police officers, and reporting to the police about dangerous incidents that may happen should occasionally be taken only after considering other options.

- Being on the scene of potential turmoil every day provides many opportunities for law enforcement officials, who should be consulted by academic researchers and analysts, to understand the details of what is happening, the motivations of all sides of confrontations, and the options for steps to prevent escalation of conflicts.

Activities of Far-Right Groups:

- It is essential to avoid simplistic responses to far-right extremism that fuels Islamist extremism.
- The radicalization process of far-right groups may be similar to radicalization of more traditional extremists even though the content of radicalization is different.
- Islamists and far-right extremists at times have used violence to provoke one another and thereby highlight their competition in recruiting new members.
- Far-right extremists have at times built local and transnational alliances based on common narratives about anti-Semitism, anti-liberalism, and anti-government.

Radicalization:

- There have been opportunities to interview thousands of prisoners in Syria and Iraq and thereby improve understanding of the radicalization and de-radicalization processes.
- Four common pieces of the puzzle in understanding radicalization are (a) the basis for grievances, (b) the ideology of the radicalized groups, (c) the relevant social and economic networks, and (d) the enabling environments that may be replete with guns, political rhetoric, interactional social media, ungoverned spaces, and/or training camps.
- Increased research on identity formation that highlights activities at an early age is needed.

Rehabilitation:

- There is a widespread need to understand the entire process of human rehabilitation, including special attention to traumatized people.

- The media should report on the details of rehabilitation activities so that the public knows they are underway.
- Failure to deal with the entire rehabilitation landscape, such as preventing access to drugs and involvements in street crime, is likely to perpetuate difficulties.

Topics for Future Inter-Academy Cooperation

Given the many organizations throughout the world that are interested in improved understanding of the dimensions of preventing and responding to violent extremism in different geographic settings, this segment of the chapter focuses on two challenges that were repeatedly raised by the participants in the NAS-RAS workshops. They are the (a) role of research and (b) future opportunities for international collaboration, including but far beyond NAS-RAS interactions.

The following research topics were highlighted as particularly important in looking forward:

- *The Role of Religion:* Doctrines and fundamental concepts among religious and seculars scholars, including comparison of religious tolerance, Koranic tolerance, and Islamic tolerance; understanding of the theology of jihad; and the roles of mosques as producers of jihad or as defenders against jihad.
- *The World of the Post-Islamist State and the Future Direction of ISIS:* Will different groups come together where possible, and where will local dynamics prevent linkages? Is there a possibility of regeneration of a terrorist structure that could become an analog of ISIS?
- *Counterterrorism Policies:* Interesting topics are comparative studies of practices in different countries, overcoming competing definitions, and encouraging greater self-reflection in responding to terrorism. How does ISIS view its adversaries? Do the actions of adversaries reinforce the core beliefs of ISIS?
- *Returnees–Particularly Women:* Priority should be given to country studies on the return of foreign fighters, attitudes of local societies, growth in right-wing reactions and retribution upon their return, and linkages among broad studies of migration from and to countries in turmoil.
- *Other Topics of Interest:* It is important to understand the impacts of local conditions and local circumstances on radicalization. The

psychology of suicide bombers remains an important field for research despite the many efforts in this area. The effectiveness of state institutions in maintaining order is a continuing issue. How important are mercenaries who engage in terrorism simply because of financial rewards?

Regarding areas for immediate international cooperation—including but well beyond NAS-RAS cooperation—the following themes were among the many topics that were proposed:

- Emphasis on drug control, periodic assessments of the nexus of drugs and violent extremism, and a focus on smuggling in Asia.
- Greater attention to transforming recommendations into policy, without losing the credibility of the academic underpinnings of such transformations.
- Future meetings involving both academics and practitioners in field assessments and control activities to help limit violent extremism, including officials associated with police activities and emergency social services personnel.
- Increased scrutiny of the many operational documents prepared by extremist groups that have become available and provide fresh insights of the motivations for and the methods of terrorism. (These documents are clarifying the approaches used on the internet and other media platforms for spreading messages of all types across large geographic areas.)
- Information warfare that will grow in importance but will go both ways, for example, countering propaganda from extremists about bombings and civilian casualties with success stories about effective cross-national cooperation.

In short, the list of topics that were considered during intensive discussions of violent extremism as viewed in different geographical settings with involvement of local experts has been impressive. Some of these topics have been discussed at other forums over many years and indeed decades.

However, few of the problems that have been cited have been completely understood; and many will persist for the foreseeable future.

THE PATHWAY AHEAD

Extremism, violence, and terrorism will continue to be on the list of challenges facing governments and populations throughout the world in the decades ahead. Scientists from the United States and Russia can contribute to the carrying out of analyses on methods to reduce the roots and blunting the trajectories of destructive acts. The NAS and the RAS have contributed to such efforts and are well positioned to continue to play a significant role of interest to the governments of the two countries.

Four of this report's appendixes are particularly important in future assessments of continuing challenges in combating deadly chaos in the years ahead.

- Appendix G: Far-Right Domestic Extremism
- Appendix H: Psychology of Transnational Terrorism
- Appendix I: Recent Trends and Future Concerns in Worldwide Terrorism
- Appendix J: Labor Migration and Radicalism

NOTES

1. Schweitzer, G. E. 2013. *Containing Russia's Nuclear Firebirds: Harmony and Change at the International Science and Technology Center.* Athens, GA: University of Georgia Press, p. 148.
2. This section is based on the record of discussions prepared during the dialogues and distributed to the participants.
3. Stepanova, E. 2017. *Addressing Terrorism: Violent Extremism and Radicalization Perspectives from the United States and Russia.* Moscow: Institute for the World Economy and International Relations. This publication includes papers prepared by participants in the first workshop that summarized their presentations.
4. NASEM (National Academies of Sciences, Engineering, and Medicine). 2017. *Improving Understanding of the Roots and Trajectories of Violent Extremism: Proceedings of a Workshop–in Brief.* Washington, DC: The National Academies Press.
   NASEM. 2019. *The Convergence of Violent Extremism and Radiological Security, Proceedings of a Workshop–in Brief.* Washington, DC: The National Academies Press.
   NASEM. 2019. *Developments in Violent Extremism in the Middle East and Beyond: Proceedings of a Workshop–in Brief.* Washington, DC: The National Academies Press.
   NASEM. 2020. *Scientific Aspects of Violent Extremism, Terrorism, and Radiological Security: Proceedings of a Workshop–in Brief.* Washington, DC: The National Academies Press.
5. Gambetta, D., and S. Hertog. 2018. *Engineers of Jihad: The Curious Connection between Violent Extremism and Education.* Princeton, NJ: Princeton University Press.

Conditions in the Arab Region

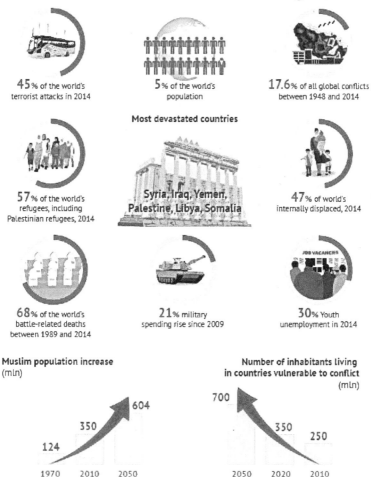

45% of the world's terrorist attacks in 2014

5% of the world's population

17.6% of all global conflicts between 1948 and 2014

Most devastated countries

57% of the world's refugees, including Palestinian refugees, 2014

Syria, Iraq, Yemen, Palestine, Libya, Somalia

47% of world's internally displaced, 2014

68% of the world's battle-related deaths between 1989 and 2014

21% military spending rise since 2009

30% Youth unemployment in 2014

Muslim population increase
(mln)

604
350
124
1970   2010   2050

Number of inhabitants living in countries vulnerable to conflict
(mln)

700
350
250
2050   2020   2010

The Arab region in figures.
Source: Vitaly Naumkin, presentation June 20, 2017, Paris, France. Based on the work of A. Aksenenok, V. Kuznetsov, V. Naumkin, N. Soukhov, I. Zvyagelskaya. The Middle East: Darkness Before the Dawn? Regional Conflicts and the Future of the Global Community. The Valdai Club. Moscow, June 2017. The data were provided by the United Nations Development Program.

6

Continuing Inter-Academy Cooperation in a Changing World

The Foreign Ministry will continue to support the inter-academy program on ethnic challenges and radiological security. Inform me or my staff if you encounter difficulties.
> – Senior Russian Foreign Ministry official during discussion in December 2019 about the most recent NAS-RAS workshop in Moscow

NAS engagement with significant Russian organizations and specialists is very important in keeping open the door until the day when the two governments can again directly engage on issues concerning radiological security.
> – Senior career program official of the U.S. Department of Energy, March 2020

We appreciate your progress in engaging the Russian ministries, and we remain supportive of your efforts.
> – Senior career policy official of the U.S. Department of State, August 2020

SETTING THE STAGE FOR FUTURE COOPERATION

In August 2020, 150 well-known American scientists and foreign policy experts, including 15 participants in National Academy of Sciences-Russian Academy of Sciences (NAS-RAS) collaborative activities that were discussed in previous chapters, urged the U.S. and Russian governments to put aside political acrimony and work together in the security and scientific arenas. These signers of a joint statement published by a respected nongovernmental organization in Washington, D.C., underscored that continuing collaborative efforts undertaken during recent years could help reduce the likelihood of armed hostilities, a concern that has been increasing. While the emphasis of the joint statement was on sustaining current commitments of the two governments to arms control agreements and on increasing international efforts that could limit the severity of climate change, the broader message was clear.

The continued loss of international leadership by the United States and Russia in supporting science-based activities of mutual interest, working both independently and together, has eroded global security in a variety of ways.[1]

This final chapter addresses the future of U.S.-Russia cooperation in important fields of security concern, building on the types of activities considered in previous chapters. It also recognizes the importance of developments in related areas appearing on the horizon. As highlighted in earlier chapters, cooperation has focused on understanding the basis for ethnic disputes leading to violence; promoting responsible biological research; encouraging enhancement of radiological security; addressing various forms of terrorism; and recognizing the political realities in assessing approaches to reduce tensions in Europe, Russia, Central Asia, and the Middle East.

Several important considerations in carrying out future terrorism-related cooperative activities are the following. Significant support by the governments of the two countries will continue to be critical in sustaining cooperation. The ease of organizing and carrying out collaboration in various locations will be crucial in attracting appropriate participants. The practical aspects of effectively involving scientists from third countries and international organizations in future NAS-RAS activities—whether they be in-person or electronic interactions—should be considered case by case.

Continuing Political Support for NAS-RAS Cooperation

As indicated in previous chapters, both governmental officials and nongovernmental specialists from many organizations have participated in inter-academy cooperation designed to improve understanding of the roots and trajectories of violent extremism and terrorism in various forms. Visas for participants in events have been issued on time. Rarely have committed scientists dropped out before the events. When they were unable to participate, the reason has almost always been "unexpected conflicts" in the scheduling of competing activities. Regarding security concerns, invited participants with ties to their governments have usually checked the appropriateness of their participation before they committed to attending scheduled events.

When considering topics that have important security dimensions, governmental limitations on participation by some scientists, particularly if meetings are not held in their home countries, have occasionally been of concern. Also, visits by foreign scientists to facilities in the United States and in Russia where classified activities are underway will continue to be difficult to organize. Even with such constraints, the NAS-RAS discussions have usually been of interest to the governments as well as to the participants.

As previously noted, cross-ocean in-person cooperation requires financial support—from governments, from foundations, from institutions of the participants, and/or from the participants themselves. The costs of Zoom interactions are quite modest; but the importance and effect of such meetings are still uncertain. Most of the activities considered in the previous chapters, which were in-person activities, were carried out with financial support by governmental organizations in one or both countries. At times, foundations and the academies themselves covered some of the expenses.

Also of importance, working jointly in the sensitive areas addressed by the academies of the two countries would not have been possible without the explicit or implicit agreement at high levels of the two governments. Fortunately, at present the governmental views in Washington and Moscow about future NAS-RAS activities related to global terrorism seem positive, even during political difficulties in the U.S.-Russian intergovernmental relationship.

Documenting Views and Suggestions of Participants in Inter-Academy Events

As previously noted, a significant characteristic of inter-academy activities considered in this report has been the participation of specialists from both countries who have had close ties with officials of their governments. These connections have eased the flow of observations and suggestions from academy venues to policy circles after completion of deliberations.

Also, the participation of well-informed and well-connected scientists has been in ensuring that discussion topics are scientifically significant and do not unknowingly duplicate related activities taking place in other venues.

A directly related lesson learned is that documentation detailing the basis for findings and conclusions during inter-academy meetings, studies, and other activities should be prepared, even if there are delays in issuing some reports. Reports, or at least summaries of reports, are most effective when they are prepared in both English and Russian.[2]

Involving Scientists from Third Countries in NAS-RAS Projects

While the NAS and the RAS were the principal organizers of the events discussed in this report, a significant number of scientists and officials from other countries also participated in some activities. This was the case for all events that were held in countries other than Russia and the United States, where local scientists also participated. During these events held in third countries, local government officials usually extended welcomes to the participants in the meetings, often highlighting activities of relevance in the region surrounding the meeting site. Also, local scientists were important participants in the activities. The importance of involving experts from other countries in future U.S.-Russian dialogues is illustrated by a 2021 European Union initiative being conducted by scientists from several countries, including Russia. This initiative will identify and support implementation of steps to improve security at religious sites that take into account the activities at a wide variety of locations across the continent, historical relationships of religious groups and group leaders with local authorities, and ingrained habits and personal aspirations among followers of different religions. Among the topics to be addressed are the following:

- Encouraging cooperation among religious leaders and security specialists in addressing evacuation procedures, safe havens within the sites, and communication and cooperation with law enforcement officials, while maintaining dignity and order within the sites.
- Adapting for use at religious sites existing guidelines for protection against chemical, biological, and high-explosion incidents; methods for recognition of unknown persons; personnel protection methods; security of irreplaceable items; and preparation of safe zones should incidents occur.

- Working with faith-based leaders in increasing awareness of threats when appropriate; improving internal communication, warning, and response requirements; and advocating appropriate procedures, behavior, and responsibilities of congregations.[3]

While the foregoing activities may seem elementary to professional security officials, incorporating them within the daily routines at religious sites must deal with beliefs dating back centuries, congregations that are skeptical about government involvement in their religious activities, and personal attitudes as to the appropriate role of governments.

THE NEXT STEPS

In early 2020 (before the spread of the COVID-19 pandemic), the NAS and the RAS agreed to organize a third workshop on the topic of extremism and radiological security during late 2020 in Moscow. The workshop has now been rescheduled for late fall 2022. The presentations and discussions by the participants are to explore in more detail than in previous workshops a few topics that were on previous agendas, along with new topics. A continuing objective of the workshop series is to develop and disseminate to the global community important perspectives on the how, why, when, and where of radiological terrorism.

Several examples of important themes—both old and new—that may be addressed during the 2022 workshop are as follows. The malevolent use of radiation-emitting sources inside shopping malls, at sports venues, and within transportation terminals deserves more attention. The feasibility of permanent disposal of liquid radioactive waste beyond simply long-term storage is difficult but of increasing importance. Concern is rapidly increasing that technological advances in drones, robots, and artificial intelligence will enhance the capabilities of terrorists to acquire and use ingredients for dirty bombs; but at the same time these technologies can be adapted to enhance the protection of radiation sources. Progress has been made in some countries in replacing the use of dangerous radiation sources—such as using cesium-137—with less dangerous approaches for medical and other purposes, but the costs of replacing such sources still inhibit broader acceptance of such steps in Russia and elsewhere.

An important objective for the 2022 workshop is to continue to expand the currently limited personal cross-ocean relationships between individuals and teams of researchers in the United States and Russia. These relationships have begun to stimulate follow-on activities undertaken at the initiative of the participants, including invitations to relevant meetings. Joint research activities and joint publications have also been discussed, but they are still largely in an incubation period.

Two steps are being considered for the 2022 workshop to underscore the importance and feasibility of cross-ocean cooperation through a variety of channels. First, a breakout group could be established to discuss how participants can pursue common interests beyond simply participating in inter-academy workshops. Of possible interest are tabletop exercises, intensive explorations of various scenarios by small teams of specialists, and group visits to facilities where emergency response teams train. Less ambitious activities by individuals might involve simply staying in touch as they prepare papers for publication based on related research endeavors.

Also looking to the future, current plans call for several graduate students from Russia and the United States to participate in the next workshop. These students will be able to describe their research activities and interim findings while also making contacts that may offer windows to future engagement.

In short, the 2022 workshop is intended to conclude the most recent series of NAS-RAS workshops focused on violence and terrorism. Discussions during the workshop should help set the stage for other topics or other forms of collaboration based on similar or different topics for future NAS-RAS programs.

EPILOGUE

"Security" considerations have always surrounded many aspects of U.S.-Russian scientific relations. This report has focused on program activities that involved security concerns. The NAS and the RAS have unique experience in working together on some of the important aspects of security and are in a position to expand their horizons in addressing the ever-emerging technological aspects of terrorism—cyber weapons, robotics, artificial intelligence, and autonomous weapons, for example.[4] At the same time, they may decide to expand their attention to the economic and human dimensions of life—particularly for engineers—in turbulent regions, including not only profiteering but also the social esteem of belonging to groups of like-minded wayward individuals.[5]

In looking ahead, this report includes 10 appendixes prepared by participants in NAS-RAS activities that address activities of both past and future importance.

- Appendixes A and B provide details on pioneering efforts to understand the drivers of ethnic violence—drivers that remain important in many areas of the world.
- Appendixes C and D provide details of terrorism acts in Moscow and the North Caucasus that remain grim reminders of the brutality of terrorism.
- Appendixes E, F, G, H, I, and J provide insights as to how the scientific communities of the United States and Russia are dealing with some of the difficult roots of terrorism.

NOTES

1. Gottemoeller, R., T. Graham, F. Hill, J. Huntsman Jr., R. Legvold, and T. R. Pickering. 2020. "It's Time to Rethink Our Russia Policy." Open letter in *Politico Magazine* (August 5).
2. Schweitzer, G. E. 2004. *Scientists, Engineers, and Track-Two Diplomacy: A Half-Century of U.S.-Russian Interacademy Cooperation.* Washington, DC: The National Academies Press, p. 88.
3. European Commission. 2020. Internal Security Fund Policies 2014–2020 (ISEP-2020-AG-Protect). https//ec.europa.eu/home-affairs/content/call-proposal-projects-isfp-2020-ag-protect_en.
4. Cronin, A. K. 2019. *Power to the People, How Open Technological Innovation Is Arming Tomorrow's Terrorists.* Oxford: Oxford University Press, p. 257.
5. Gambetta, D., and S. Hertog. 2018. *Engineers of Jihad: The Curious Connection between Violent Extremism and Education.* Princeton, NJ: Princeton University Press, p. 159.

BAIKAL REGION
- 55,000 inhabitants
- Environmentally Protected
- Reduced Radiophobia

Alternate Variations of Long-Term Storage
(US-Russia Studies)
US-Russia Cooperation in Assessing
Permanent Waste Disposal

Cooperation in long-term storage and waste disposal.
Source: Presentation by Vladimir Petrov, 2019.

Visit by American and European scientists to RADON radiological waste facility,
December 2019.
Source: Photo by host.

Appendix A

The Kona Statement

This appendix includes excerpts from the Kona Statement, which was prepared in Kona, Hawaii, in 1994 by a U.S.-led international team of scholars from the United States, Russia, and Eastern Europe. It served as an important basis for contributions by Valery Tishkov and other discussants during National Academy of Sciences–Russian Academy of Sciences meetings in 1999–2004 due to its continued relevance to developments within Russia and other former states of the Soviet Union for many years.

MANAGING ETHNIC CONFLICT

Ethnic or "national" identity and the struggle for ethnic self-determination have often played two quite different roles in modern history. They have been a major force in the decline of imperialism, totalitarianism, and enforced ideology and thus in the expansion of human rights and freedoms while being the basis for the recovery and strengthening of individual dignity. On the other hand, they have been the source of corrosive tensions and destructive conflicts, leading to the deaths of millions of people and to huge material losses, blocking economic and political reform, and serving as a justification for violations of human rights and the imposition of oppressive regimes....

For centuries, problems arose in places where migration and political change resulted in communities of minorities that had different ethnic identities or national traditions. The minority and majority communities clashed over their relative access to natural resources; national wealth; social, political, and economic positions; and educational opportunities....

In the life of a multiethnic state, relations among its constituted communities may seem normal, and little or nothing is done to deal with the possibility of future conflict. Yet, constructive measures can be taken at this stage to prevent the eruption of such conflicts. The objective at this stage should be to foster inclusion and full citizenship for all. There should be an attempt to enlarge the participation of ethnic minorities in public decision-making so as to enhance their confidence that their rights are being respected and that they can rely on fair treatment by public authorities. Newly independent states should accept the "zero" variant of citizenship. All persons living on the territory of the state at the moment of its establishment are entitled to be full citizens. Electoral systems and political parties should be organized in ways that encourage ethnic coalitions.

Social and economic policies should seek to improve the conditions and status of groups that have been the victims of discrimination and to enlarge their opportunities, although experience in the United States and India suggests that "reverse discrimination" may be counterproductive....

The education system should be encouraged to include instruction about the fallacy and peril of ethnic prejudice and the duty of individuals to be alert to their own tendencies to engage in ethnic stereotyping. Special educational efforts should be directed to traditionally disadvantaged ethnic groups to improve their ability to define their own interests, responsibilities, and possibilities in the larger society and to assume positions of political and economic leadership at both local and national levels. Individuals and organizations in the mass media should be encouraged to assume responsibility for carefully investigating and verifying accounts of ethnic threats or confrontations before publicizing them. But efforts to outlaw the public expressions of ethnic prejudice are not always effective. Indeed, the trial of those charged with violating such statutes can sometimes give rise to heightened tensions....

There is no reason to assume that ethnic tensions will inevitably develop into overt hostilities; but it is all too common that they do, often resulting from neglect of the measures that could have been taken during the latency stage. The more obvious warning swings of these shifts are (a) increased accusation of wrongdoing by ethnic groups and references to ethnic stereotypes in public discussion and political discourse, (b) the appearance of rumors of atrocities supposedly perpetrated by one ethnic group or another, and (c) demands for extraordinary steps to benefit or "protect" the majority or minority groups or to restrict the liberties of those believed to threaten these groups....

Privatization of the economies of the former communist countries has often contributed to ethnic tensions, because groups that make their living through trading can readily be perceived as profiting "illegitimately" from the market system and other aspects of economic reform. This has happened in Moscow and in Eastern Europe. These processes may then erupt in sporadic incidents of ethnic violence. At that point, the government must move promptly to maintain order and authority; and it must make clear its rejection of violence as a mode of political action, including violence by an element of the national majority or of a politically dominant minority....

The most immediate need is for strengthened measures to maintain public order. It is, of course, essential that these be seen as free of ethnic bias. An impartially commanded, highly disciplined, and ethnically mixed police force that is trained in techniques of crowd and riot control is vital. The police and customs authorities should closely monitor and control the movement of arms within the country, including those imported from abroad; and they should do whatever is possible to interdict the circulation of incendiary propaganda....

It is extremely important to foster accurate, unbiased information and communication, particularly in the mass media. A program should be in place to totally expose and discredit rumors. Journalists and editors should be aware of their ethical and professional responsibilities. Instant and severe reaction to calls for violence, ethnic libel, and other acts breaching the proper limits of free expression is essential, not only to do justice but to make it evident to the public that justice is being done. Inflammatory or libelous statements or claims should be promptly answered by public authorities....

At this stage, too, governments need to understand the international implications of their actions. Their countries' ability to control, if not prevent, ethnic violence fundamentally affects the treatment they receive from international institutions and from the foreign investment community....

A first imperative is to stop any fighting, or at least control it in a politically sensitive way, with a view toward the ultimate achievement of a constructive outcome. The instigators of violent acts should be detained or arrested, or at any rate removed from the sites of conflict. The forces of order must be well disciplined and under effective political control. If local police are suspected of harboring technically biased sentiments, it may be useful to bring in non-local police forces. Responsible control of communications and taking into account the objectives of the mass media are very important.

Then, of course, mechanisms for obtaining cease-fires and initiating negotiation are essential. All the while, the influence of international business in supporting moderate forces should not be neglected, for the economy of any country is affected by the goodwill and the investment decisions of actors in the international business community....

Sooner or later, the conflict must end, and it will be necessary to reconstruct a civil order from the wreckage left by the ethnic struggle. The parties to the struggle must be reconciled and the claims of victory must be adjusted to the realities of the continued national functioning and the necessities of continued ethnic coexistence....

Unfortunately, it is often true that the militias responsible for the violence are made into heroes and thereby reap political benefits. Whenever possible, international pressure should be exerted to prevent them from assuming national leadership in the post-conflict situation. Public debate should be encouraged with the aim of promoting positive change. The conflict should be de-dramatized, its events should not be allowed to become the "stuff" of sacred memory, and any concept of "blood revenge" should be denounced....

The goal should be to return the nation to an early stage with conflict contained. The possibility then exists that with proper steps—vigorously carried out and informed by experience—durable universally beneficial, peaceful relationships can be established among the nation's diverse ethnic groups.

Appendix B

Characteristics of Early Ethnic Monitoring Network in Russia and Beyond

The following general indicators of the state of ethno-political relationships were developed and distributed as the format for annual surveys across many regions of Russia and other parts of the former Soviet Union for two decades (beginning in the mid-1990s). The surveys were designed to assist evaluations of the sociopolitical situation in more than 50 states or regions. They often triggered actions to help restrain and/or reduce ethnic animosities.

1. *Environment and Resources:* Suitable water, soil resources, natural wealth, technological influences, and disasters and catastrophes.
2. *Demography and Migration:* Resettlement, mixed marriages and divorces, natural movements of populations, and mechanized movements of populations.
3. *Power, State, and Politics:* State administrative status, doctrine and regime of power, ethnic representation, relations between the center of the region/country/municipality and the periphery, human rights and collective rights, social order and control over weapons, and legal investigations with the implementation of court decisions.
4. *Economics and the Social Sphere:* Production and dynamics of prices, income level and disparity of income, employment and unemployment, distribution of labor, socio-professional mobility, participation in privatization and sale of land, state of social protection, and crime and communal violence.

5. *Culture, Education, and Information:* Cultural domination, religious life, language status, primary and secondary education, higher education, mass media, traditional holidays and rituals, and historical discourse.

6. *Contacts and Stereotypes:* Group demands and complaints, previous conflicts and collective traumas, ethnic stereotypes, change in self-consciousness, myths, fear and rumors, presence of group ideas and ideologies, and level of tolerance.

7. *External Conditions:* Presence and influence of diasporas, stability/ instability of neighboring and bordering regions and countries, influence of global rivalry, territorial claims and problems of borders, external connections and cooperation, and changing external image.

Additional details on the definition of the terms used above and the process of aggregating and weighing different factors are set forth in other documents. The important aspect of this network was establishing a foundation for many important conversations between local government officials/ journalists/ethnic group leaders and the aggrieved minority parties. The surveys provided important openings for discussions of issues in their early stages.

Source: Tishkov, V. A. 2003. "The Dynamic Factors of Ethno-Political Conflicts in Post-Soviet States," in *Conflict and Reconstruction in Multiethnic Societies: Proceedings of a Russian-American Workshop.* Washington, DC: The National Academies Press.

Appendix C

Lessons Learned from a Terrorist Attack in a Moscow Theater

Yevgeny Kolesnikov
Russian Federal Security Service

This is a portion of a report prepared by the Russian government pursuant to a request from the National Academy of Sciences for an authoritative governmental perspective on the attack. It was widely accepted by Russian and American terrorism experts as a reasonable account of the horrific incident and provides important details of key issues that had previously been controversial.

On October 23, 2002, a band of terrorists led by Chechen field commander Movsar Barayev seized the Palace of Culture of the Moscow Ball-Bearing Factory, where more than 920 people were attending a performance of the musical *Nord-Ost*. The Russian government immediately set up an operations center involving many government agencies near the site to oversee the government's response and to keep the public informed as the incident unfolded. The operations center ascertained the existence of a facility with a physical structure identical to the structure of the Palace of Culture that provided a base for practicing for an operation at the Palace.

Initially, storming of the building to rescue the hostages was not seen as the only option. The preferred approach by the operations center was to remove the terrorists on the basis of negotiations. As the result of initial negotiations, several groups of hostages were released, including some children under the age of 10. Also, after a careful search for hiding places in the external walls of the Palace and emergence of other routes out of the

Palace, 113 people were safe before the security services eventually stormed the building. This included 69 who escaped and 44 who were rescued.

All the while, the terrorists were pressuring the hostages through various forms of psychological fear. For example, the terrorists successfully demanded that relatives of some of the hostages organize and attend protest demonstrations in Moscow calling for the withdrawal of Russian troops from Chechnya and the granting of independence to the republic. But agreement on a peaceful ending of the standoff was not at hand. Four hostages were then shot, and the chance of a peaceful outcome was reduced to zero.

At that time, 35 to 40 terrorists were holding the hostages in the auditorium of the Palace. Powerful explosive devices had been placed in the center of the hallway and in the balcony of the auditorium, with mines put on the stage aimed at the audience. Fifteen to 18 female suicide bombers wearing belts with explosive devices were deployed around the perimeters of the auditorium and in the center of the seating area.

The forward deployment of the government assault teams was preceded by release into the building of special Fentanyl–based gas that had been widely used during surgery in Russia and in other countries. It was known to facilitate temporary reduction of movements of patients without threatening their lives or health.

During the special operation that followed, 41 fighters under the command of the Chechen field leader were killed. More than 750 hostages were freed, including 60 foreigners. However, while emergency medical assistance was provided to all hostages who needed assistance, 129 died, including 8 foreigners. Russian health-care specialists had accurately predicted that there would be some deaths from stress, hypodynamia, hunger, dehydration, and exacerbation of preexisting illnesses.

The arsenal of weapons available to the terrorists was extensive. It included 76 kilograms of explosives, 17 automatic rifles, 20 hand guns, 25 homemade explosive devices, many suicide belts, 2 homemade bombs in the form of metallic tanks filled with artillery shells, 106 grenades, and more than 5,000 rounds of ammunition.

Evidence gathered during investigation of the incident included documentation of repeated attempts to force the Russian leadership to hold talks with the leadership of the rebels in Chechnya. A prerecorded message that was broadcast by Al Jazeera was found. Telephone calls to force relatives of hostages to sign appeals to the Russian president were uncovered. A well-developed press campaign in parallel with the incident was also discovered.

The Russian government had considerable difficulties in working with the media during the event. Some journalists covered the event in a tendentious manner and used the activity for their own particular aims. The Russian government underscored that it must continue to work with journalists in improving relations during such situations.

Russia is ready to do everything in its power to (a) disseminate the experience it has gained in conducting such hostage rescue operations, (b) exchange information on the weapons and equipment used, and (c) organize joint training exercises for both command and special operations units.

Finally, the evidence that was gathered during the investigation of the incident illustrated the link between this crime and the designs of the ideologists of international terrorists who plan and finance broad-scale terrorism acts throughout the world. The methods used in implementing the preparatory phase and in the act of hostage taking were characteristic of those used by extremists organizations associated with al-Qaeda, the Taliban, and other criminal groups espousing terrorism and violence as a means to achieving their goals. Also at the national level, expert assessments have established that the types of homemade explosives devices used both in the *Nord-Ost* incident and a car bombing at a McDonald's restaurant in Moscow a few months earlier were identical.

For additional information: Kolesnikov, Y. A. 2004. "Lessons Learned from the *Nord-Ost* Terrorist Attack in Moscow from the Standpoint of Russian Security and Law Enforcement Agencies," in *Terrorism: Reducing Vulnerabilities and Improving Responses: U.S.-Russian Workshop Proceedings*. Washington, DC: The National Academies Press.

Appendix D

Terrorist Attack at a School in the North Caucasus

Gennady Kovalenko
Russian Federal Security Service

This is a portion of a report prepared by the Russian government pursuant to a request from the National Academy of Sciences for an authoritative government perspective on the attack. It was widely accepted by Russian and American terrorism experts as a reasonable account of the horrific incident and provided important details of key issues that had been controversial.

In 2004 there was a sharp increase in terrorism in Russia, culminating in the devastating events in Beslan. It was the year of the presidential election, so the results of Vladimir Putin's first term were being debated. The Chechen public election was also held in 2004 and was supposed to consolidate the republic's turn toward a peaceful life. At the same time, this was also the year of the 60th anniversary of the forced departure of tens of thousands of people of the Caucasus to distant lands. Chechen fighters marked such important dates with bloody acts.

At the same time, there were other reasons for increased terrorist activities. For example, the numerous terrorist attacks, sabotage, murders, and abductions during 1998–2004 did not lead to any politically significant changes, with serious complaints against the leaders of the bandit groups by their foreign financial sponsors. To prove their professional suitability, the revolutionary leaders in Chechnya felt that they had to carry out a series of brutal terrorist acts, as described below. In February there was a metro explosion in Moscow killing 39 people and wounding 350 others.

In May in Grozny, an explosive device was detonated at an outdoor concert killing seven people, including Chechen President Akhmad Kadyrov. In June, 300 Chechen bandits took control of two towns in Ingushetia. In August, 300 armed bandits set up checkpoints on the roads in Grozny and for 3 hours attacked police stations in various parts of the city with fatalities including 25 police officers and ordinary citizens. In August, a terrorist attack at Domodedovo Airport in Moscow led to crashes of two airliners with the death of 90 crew members and passengers. Shortly thereafter, a suicide bomber killed 10 people and wounded 50 more at a Moscow metro station.

Then bandits in the North Caucasus, in constant contact with Middle East compatriots, particularly in the United Arab Emirates, headed for Beslan, bringing an arsenal of weapons, equipment, and explosive devices with them. After learning of their seizure of hostages at the Beslan school, police blocked off access to the school, and Russian troops from the Ministry of the Interior arrived. Within the cordoned-off area, the ministry immediately focused on locating the hostages in a complex area of buildings where the school was located.

A large number of hostages were held in the gym, while groups of 100 or more were in other school buildings. All locations had been mined, and the authorities quickly concluded that it would not be possible to disarm the mines since they would be detonated automatically if not under terrorist control. Also, a significant number of the invaders were under the influence of narcotics. The criminals limited contact with the outside and killed 21 people the first day, while denying water or food of any kind to the remainder.

The authorities tried to negotiate with the invaders, bringing in well-known personalities from the region to assist. Fortunately, 216 mothers and children were released. Additional local residents were then brought in to also participate in the negotiations, and the authorities offered to exchange prisoners from previous engagements for the release of additional hostages. They offered a monetary ransom with the promise of return of the bandits to Chechnya unimpeded. At the same time, the terrorists requested sovereignty for Chechnya and the removal of all federal troops from the republic.

Suddenly, two explosions took place in the gymnasium, and fire broke out. Reportedly, the terrorists were intoxicated and apparently lost control of the explosive devices. In the panic that followed, some hostages attempted to run from the building and were shot. The security services then undertook the task of systematically evacuating the hostages while killing the terrorists. This task was complicated by the sudden involvement of local residents with arms also entering the fray. Freeing the hostages and destroying the terrorists took more than 10 hours.

A total of 330 people were killed at Beslan, including 186 children; and 31 terrorists were killed. No terrorists managed to hide. One was arrested, and he was from Chechnya. The subsequent investigation quickly identified 17 of the terrorists, including their leader who resided in Chechnya but was an Ingushetian by nationality. Others could not be quickly identified. Five police officers were promptly accused of negligence, and six individuals were soon arrested for aiding the terrorists.

The events in Beslan, the armed attacks in Ingushetia and Grozny in the summer of 2004, and the terrorist attacks in Moscow were all part of a unified strategy of the ideologues of international terrorism to expand their influence as widely as possible, create an atmosphere of universal fear, cause the population to mistrust the capabilities of the government, and force the government leaders to enter into negotiations with bandit leaders. The leaders of the Chechen fighters continued making focused efforts to spread instability not only to Chechnya but also to the majority of adjoining territories.

As the Russian leadership quickly acknowledged, the economic picture in the North Caucasus region remained pitiful; therefore, the region was simultaneously a victim of the bloody terror and a platform for its replication. The roots of terrorism were the result of massive unemployment and the lack of an effective social policy.

Several measures were promptly taken following the events in Beslan.

- A presidential commission was created to prevent and suppress terrorist acts and to detect and eliminate the causes and conditions that allowed them to be planned and carried out. Operational antiterrorism management groups were formed in all regions of the Southern Federal District. They were assigned the task of coordinating all military and law enforcement activities in the region.
- The State Duma addressed the region's socioeconomic problems, which were linked to 40 existing laws. One important legal change called for the military authorities to counter terrorism not only by force but also with the law, involving all government agencies. Leadership in countering terrorism was given to the Federal Security Service.
- Mechanisms for promoting economic development were established with emphasis on activities such as transportation, hydroelectric

power, traditional agriculture, enterprises of the military-industrial complex, and ecotourism.

- In the sphere of international cooperation, more active participation in U.N. activities, deliberations of G-8 countries, activities of the NATO-Russia Council, the Organization for Security and Co-operation in Europe, and the Council for Europe was encouraged.

U.S.-Russia cooperation was considered essential, including strengthening control over trade of weapons, extradition of terrorists, and closing channels for financing of terrorist organizations. This cooperation could be linked to a timely analysis of experience of many countries, particularly the United States, in the struggle against terrorists. Who is to blame? How did such an event become possible? What must change? What recommendations will promote success for specific issues facing Russia?

For additional information: Kovalenko, G. 2006. "On the Events in Beslan," in *Countering Urban Terrorism in Russia and the United States: Proceedings of a Workshop.* Washington, DC: The National Academies Press.

Appendix E

New Trends in
Monitoring Multiethnic Russia

Academician Valery Tishkov
Institute for Ethnography and Anthropology

The aim of ethnologic monitoring is to provide a basis for the analysis of trends in the cultural and religious "superdiversity" of Russian society from the viewpoints of risks and nationwide consensus. The objective is to find an answer to this question: Does the Russian population's cultural complexity embody a national weakness and a barrier to successful development, or is it unrelated to stability and welfare and can it even become a potential resource for development? And a related question: What are the meaning and mechanisms of nation-building in contemporary Russia?

The situation with national consolidation of the new country's citizens is complicated due both to the historic cataclysm of the Soviet Union's collapse and to the new geopolitical competitions and continuing institutionalization of ethnicity in the federal system (22 ethnogeographic autonomous republics). This situation, in turn, has produced and is now feeding a primordial vision of ethnicity at both the population's everyday level and the level of experts. Ethnonationalism also remains in the foundations of national construction of all the countries of the former Soviet Union; and given ineffective governance, internal crises, or external effects, there are serious widespread risks of conflicts and even disintegration. The 2020 amendments to the Russian Federation Constitution do not reflect the concept of nation-building based on a multiethnic civil nation while retaining the Soviet formula of a multinational people and even exacerbating that formula with a new record of a "nation-forming people," meaning ethnic Russians. This has been a step back from the ratification of all-Russian identity and the post-Soviet concept of a civil or political Russian nation along with today's self-identification, which underscores "we are the Russian people, the citizens of the Russian Federation."

This conservative trend was caused primarily by internal power dispositions, but it also partially reflects the global trend of a crisis for liberalism and the very concept of a nation-state. In Russia, this concept is disputed by conservative political forces and the expert community (including the Russian Orthodox Church), which advance the alternative thesis that Russia is a unique civilization. Thus, *a doctrinal-scale question is added to the analytics monitoring repertoire, namely, what is the "Russian idea" and what is the basis for Russia's nationhood.*

Russia is subject to multidirectional centralization and regional-ethnic disintegration factors. On the one hand, nationwide institutions (the Constitution and federal government, power structures, the education system, the army, the national Russian language and Russian-speaking media, the professional culture, etc.) promote the formation of a shared civic identity. On the other hand, the existence of ethnonational institutions in the republics and the preservation and support of particular ethnic cultures shape an ethnic identity among the non-Russian population, according to its importance in certain situations. This applies especially to so-called titular nations. This primacy could spill over into interethnic contradictions and rejection of the shared state.

A mirror-image situation exists in cultural and political manifestations on behalf of the dominant majority—ethnic Russians whose identity is expressed powerfully and in many ways, beginning with the historical narrative, language, and religion, and ending with the name of the country. We cannot deny that the "political" Russian bias exists because there is an "ethnic" Russian bias. Of course in Russia, that is the core culture that is the starting point of the country's nationality and strength. However, under certain conditions, mobilization of the "ethnic" Russian factor can entail as many risks as those of peripheral nationalism or separatism. It would seem that Russians are inseparable from anyone, and they are the first custodians of nationality; but we must not forget 1991, when "ethnic/political Russia" in the form of the Russian Soviet Federative Socialist Republic was one of the initiators of the fall of the Soviet Union. Thus, *not only ethnic minorities but also advocates of radicalism on behalf of the majority require regular monitoring.*

In the recent decade religion, which plays a role that varies, has become a factor in the formation of group identities and a subject of monitoring. In some cases, religion blurs ethnic boundaries; in others, to the contrary, it reinforces ethnic identity, making ethnic group boundaries more rigid. On the whole, religion should be a source of stability and reconciliation unless radical/fundamentalist projects and forces arise in or around its environment. Our analysis shows that dialogue and mutual respect and a willingness to cooperate with the state exist at the level of religious leaders. However, conflict situations form at the level of church-affiliated and religiously motivated activists and in response to public moods. Conflicts and incidents of violence occur around (a) property and construction of churches, (b) the status of places of worship, (c) the importance of public services, and (d) debates over symbols of faith. Government agencies rather successfully neutralize the forces of international terrorism on the country's territory and prevent terrorist acts, but this does not guarantee the elimination of religiously motivated conflicts, especially when ethnic group boundaries align with faith boundaries. From this standpoint, *the religious situation is an interesting field both for study and monitoring and for the development of models of the regulation of interfaith relations and religious policy.*

Ethnicity and religion shape cultural aspects of world vision and patterns of behavior, which are often described in terms of "national character," "traditional values," or "ethnic stereotypes." At the same time, civic integration resulting from purposeful efforts by the intellectual elite, governmental institutions, and everyday human practices leads to reinforcement of the shared national culture with its values and symbols commonly understood by all. This process relies on interactive experience of members of various cultures and belief systems within the historic Russian nation-state. But this same process implies the need for sociocultural innovations and "big projects" as conditions for development. For this reason, an attempt by some experts to lay the foundation for an understanding of Russia and its image of a future concept by a special "civilization code" with a set of eternal mythological characteristics entails a risk of arrogant isolationism and exceptionalism and of rejection of the culturally complex nature of Russian society.

During the ethnologic monitoring of recent years, studies have examined the relationship and interaction of the shared national (Russian) culture with ethnic and religious traditions, values, and norms: how they are combined, whether they are capable of integration and peaceful coexistence, or whether they are doomed as adherents of the tenets of "incompatibility of cultures" and "collision of civilizations" believe. Our hypothesis rests on the idea that the cultural ideals, values, and self-consciousness (identity) together with the feelings of engagement with the country and its people are all an important resource for development and effective governance. At the same time, the culture is inhomogeneous and variable, subject to interpretation, and the person's and citizen's identity is not only the ideas and attitudes conferred and taught by the family and educational environment, but is also an arena for competition among various influences and prescriptions, including external destructive influences. Thus, *the problem of indoctrination through modern influence systems becomes one of the keys in ensuring civic, faith, and interethnic peace and consensus.* The recent radical changes in relations among people of different ethnicities under the influence of events in Georgia, Ukraine, and Belarus, and media propaganda and social networks require expansion of the parameters of ethno-monitoring.

We believe that much depends on the person himself and on his internal resources, attitudes, and thoughts. But these attitudes depend on a series of social, cultural, and psychological factors. The defining factor in ensuring the interethnic consensus and stability of multiethnic communities is national policy and the effect of powerful institutions of civil society. So an important area for monitoring is the study that includes (a) how nationwide, ethnic, and religious identities are shaped in contemporary Russia; (b) what factors affect this process; (c) how these factors interact; (d) what meaning people invest in the concepts of nation and faith, and what roles these identities play in various areas of life (public and private life, cultural and religious needs, work and home arenas, etc.); and (e) whether they are equally important in the same domains of human existence.

How are the images of the "ethnic culture" of the greater and lesser Motherland shaped, what do these images include, and what do they mean for the citizens themselves? What role do bilingual capability and cultural complexity play at the collective and individual levels? Can a shared national identity in a multicultural state have some components of a single cultural-historic basis? If so, what should that basis be? Does it require development of a historic myth (a grand narrative), and how can general concerns be combined with particular interests? To solve these problems, analyses must focus on ethnic and religious symbols and their interpretations, forms of symbolic behavior, the meaning of the language-factor, social memory and images of the past, images of the country and other ideas throughout the world, and the religious understanding of the meaning of life and its combination with scientific approaches. The big question is "the battle for the past," including the changes in the present situation and intentional falsifications of history.

One object of study is cultural-religious intolerance and xenophobia, racism, and neofascism based on intolerance. To date, *the paths of recruitment to the ideology and practice of extremist violence, generally of young citizens of diverse social backgrounds and psychological makeups,* have not been studied. What life values are opposed to the phenomenon of "wars of liberation" that feed terrorism?

In the 1990s, attention of researchers turned to status-type conflicts (sovereignty, self-determination, autonomy, etc.) and to problems of religious revival and rehabilitation of punished people. Today, attention to conflict is shifting to social entitlements and allocation of resources, to material and political-ideological issues, to collision of lifestyles, and to geopolitical games. *In this new situation, divisive conflicts and alienation between human communities (peoples) can arise from small cultural differences, as is happening, for example, between the Russian and Ukrainian peoples.* These new circumstances require fundamental scientific analysis.

Appendix F

Final Stages in
Disposition of Radioactive Waste

Academician Vladislav A. Petrov
Institute of Geology of Ore Deposits, Petrography,
Mineralogy, and Geochemistry

This report highlights the importance of continued National Academy of Sciences–Russian Academy of Sciences cooperation in addressing the challenges of the final stages of disposal of radioactive material.

A consensus-based solution to the problems during the final stages of nuclear materials management is an important challenge for Russia and the United States, especially in view of radiological risks at low levels of exposure. Cooperation between the Russian Academy of Sciences (RAS) and the National Academy of Sciences (NAS) in this field has a very good "credibility history." In 2003 the National Academies Press issued the report *End Points for Spent Nuclear Fuel and High-Level Radioactive Waste in Russia and the United States.* The report was written by leading specialists from the two countries, including John F. Ahearne, Nikolai P. Laverov, Rodney C. Ewing, B. John Garrick, Darleane C. Hoffman, Nikolay N. Melnikov, Boris F. Myasoedov, Alexander A. Pek, Michail I. Solonin, Yuri K. Shiyan, and others.

The study that led to the report was supported by the U.S. Department of Energy. The report provides scientific and technical analyses on handling of spent nuclear fuel (SNF) and high-level radioactive waste (HLW) and the associated management challenges in Russia and the United States. The report provides characteristics of the content of wastes, comparative analyses of management approaches adopted in the two countries, and evaluations of different options for the final stages of interim and long-term storage of materials and waste, as well as final disposal of waste. The final phase for damaged SNF and nonrecyclable HLW calls for creation of disposal conditions that set a stage for a stable, secure, and reliable location for these materials, thereby preventing their access by extremists and professional terrorists.

The consolidated information has helped in correctly assessing all possible actions that should be adopted by Russia and the United States from both the near-term and the long-term perspectives. New areas of cooperation for solving the problems of interest for the two countries were also identified. These areas include the following:

1. Training highly qualified personnel now and in the future.
2. Protecting nuclear materials by locating them at a few reliably protected facilities.
3. Conducting research and development of methodologies for anti-terrorism measures.
4. Upgrading technology and approaches for handling SNF discharges, including utilization of decommissioned nuclear power stations.
5. Managing waste generated during production of nuclear weapons.
6. Transporting SNF.
7. Developing high-stability matrices for immobilization of various types of HLW.
8. Developing integrated approaches for selection of the geological environment and locations for long-term storage and disposal of nuclear materials.
9. Improving methods of processing SNF and HLW.

This pioneering work was the foundation for a number of joint research activities within such frameworks as "An International Repository of Irradiated Nuclear Fuel. Investigation of Possibilities for Establishing a Nuclear Waste Repository in Russia" (NAP, 2005); "Prospects for Improving Nuclear Safety. Protection of Weapons-Grade Materials in Russia" (NAP, 2006); "Preparatory work for Establishment of International Storage Facilities for Spent Nuclear Fuel" (2008, NAP); and "Internationalization of the Nuclear Fuel Cycle: Goals, Strategy, and Challenges" (2009, NAP).

To deal with the problem of final stages of handling nuclear materials, Russia has recently undertaken significant efforts. For example, intensive development of construction of a deep disposal facility for radioactive waste in Nizhnekanskii Granitoid Massive, in the Mountain-Chemical Combine area (Zheleznogorsk, Krasnoyarsk region) is underway. A comprehensive research program to substantiate long-term security of nuclear waste disposal based on optimization of operational parameters was developed to implement the project during 2016–2018. "The Strategic Masterplan of Research to Substantiate Security of Construction, Exploitation and Closing of Deep Disposal Site for Radioactive Waste" has been approved by the State Atomic Energy Corporation (SAEC), which is linked to ROSATOM. Also, another relevant document is "The Strategy to Construct a Deep Disposal Facility for Radioactive Waste." It sets forth the planning of events for more than 50 years into the future.

The challenge in approaching the final stages of nuclear materials handling and secure isolation of SNF—accumulated and routinely formed—continues to be a major radio-ecological problem in Russia. Many repositories are already full in accordance with their design levels or are very close to such a state. Thus, SAEC ROSATOM is constructing and plans to construct more new facilities. In this regard, the territory of the Priargunsk Mining and Chemical Association (PAO PPGHO), which is the biggest uranium ore mining and processing enterprise in Russia, is very promising because of its geographical location, natural and geological conditions, and infrastructure, economic, and technological opportunities for establishing an SNF repository, which can be given international status. The enterprise is situated in East Transbaikalia, where molybdenum-uranium is exploited in the Streltsovsk ore field.

This district is located in a sparsely populated area at a significant distance from large towns, settlements, and industrial centers. Also, it is connected with other Russian regions by railroad lines, roadways, and airline routes. The area is known for its detailed geological characteristics, which resulted from years of prospecting and exploration, geological and geophysical surveys, exploratory drilling and underground mining, and extensive scientific research work.

Crystalline rocks are present in the Archean-Proterozoic gneisses and Paleozoic granites, which are massive rocks with high strength properties in an undisturbed state. There are slightly deformed geological blocks, which due to their sizes can comprise the infrastructure of an underground SNF facility. Different variants of such a facility have been discussed with specialists from a U.S. National Research Council committee, led by M. Levenson and C. McCombie. They visited PAO PPGHO in 2002 to study problems associated with the final stages of nuclear material management in Russia.

It is clear that both the United States and Russia can solve many problems with the treatment of nuclear materials independently. But new challenges and the urgent need to reduce even low levels of radiological risks dictate the importance of further cooperative research that was started by the RAS and the NAS to manage the problems during the final stages in handling nuclear materials.

Appendix G

Far-Right Domestic Extremism

James Halverson, Senior Faculty Specialist
U.S. National Consortium for the Study of Terrorism and
Responses to Terrorism

This warning in January 2021 about the far-right extremism in the United States and Russia by a member of the National Academy of Sciences team suggests possible new priorities in future U.S.-Russian exchanges on security-related issues.

Terrorism has represented a rare area of shared security interest between the United States and Russia since September 11, 2001; and exchanges between U.S. and Russian scholars on issues of terrorism has shown to be a durable forum for security dialogue, even when formal diplomatic relations have been strained. At the time of this writing, however, the United States faces rising far-right domestic extremist movements, some of which threaten to engage in concerted anti-government violence. This shift does not provide the practical basis for U.S. and Russian counterterrorism alignment that transnational religious terrorism once did; but it does raise many questions about processes of radicalization, around which continued scholarly exchange can be oriented.

Violence perpetrated in service of extreme nativist and ethnonationalist ideologies has represented the dominant form of terrorist violence in the United States for the last decade. Data also suggests that per capita, homicides committed under far-right political motives have been even more common in Russia over a similar time frame. Although the far-right terrorist threat is real in both countries, the different cultural contexts and political implications in each country limit the productivity of international dialogue that focuses on its manifestations. Instead, a focus on the mechanisms of radicalization and their evolution in the internet age might offer common points of interest and understanding, to which separate national experiences and a wider range of disciplines can be brought to bear. Exchange on this topic might also serve interstate stability, given the dangerous capacity for online mechanisms of domestic radicalization to be harnessed as tools of interstate competition.

From the American perspective—having witnessed political polarization occur with incredible scale and speed in recent years—the current radicalization problem requires new examinations of human behavior and information technologies; but most critically, it demands better understanding of the ways these two aspects interact on a societal scale. As someone young enough to be considered a "digital native" but also old enough to remember the bright predictions made in the infancy of the internet about its potential to be a connecting force, I feel comfortable asserting that the general effect of the internet on societies in the early 2020s is not toward richer dialogue or greater inter-demographic understanding. Instead, the social dimensions of the internet, collectively dubbed "social media," constitute a distributed broadcast medium that primarily promotes declaration.

Of course, such a medium can and does have many positive impacts. In reality, however, it is also proving to be full of perverse incentives encouraging of greater social tribalism. In a social environment where each individual is a broadcaster, dialogue is rare. What dominates instead are contests for attention. In this environment, sensational, controversial, and extreme content is the easiest way to win attention. As in terrorist violence committed to win attention, the extreme is continually normalized and motives for escalation and outbidding emerge. Simultaneously, the underlying machinery of social media platforms is designed to maximize usage time and activity by learning users' preferences and steering them toward compatible content. The effect of this is the accretion of users into ideologically homogeneous orbits that are capable of drifting far from the mainstream while remaining largely unaware or unappreciative of their collective drift. Finally, owing to the accessibility and the addictive qualities of social media platforms, they create vicious cycles whereby the more content users generate, the more capable their corner of the internet is of dominating their awareness. Compounding the problem, individuals who are already at higher risk of radicalization due to economic or social deprivation may be the most prone to envelopment in radicalizing online echo chambers.

In the United States, it appears that these processes have significantly accelerated political polarization. They have also proven capable of pulling partially compatible but previously disconnected groups—like militant ethnonationalists and extreme conspiracy theorists—together and collectively toward greater radicalization. At the time of this writing, it is not clear if these enlarged extremist environments online will translate into a correspondingly elevated period of political violence. There are many warnings that it will. It is possible that the abundant availability of attention online will supplant some of the impetus to commit spectacular acts of terrorism (i.e., acts of violence to attain an audience), but it seems equally possible that assured publicity will empower more radicals to engage in some level of expressive violence. Finally, to fully grasp the present and future security implications of social media-enabled radicalization, it will be critical to investigate the degree to which the global COVID-19 pandemic—particularly the social and economic deprivations it has wrought—has increased susceptibility to online radicalization. Evidence about this from experience in the United States is mostly anecdotal at this stage, but it is compelling and supported by prior studies of radicalization drivers.

Although some of these ills may seem like uniquely American problems, their makings are not. These radicalizing processes, which appear to have gripped the political right wing in recent years, are not confined to that side of the political spectrum or to the United States. In the United States, understanding the darker aspects of the gestalt entity of internet and society is urgent because demystifying the radicalization process is an important part of creating "off-ramps" for the radicalized. Even in places where these problems are less urgent, however, most of the same ingredients for runaway cycles of polarization exist and are at least beginning to stoke entrenchment of identity politics or otherwise amplify social cleavages.

Adapting as individuals and countries to the information age will be a long-term, largely reactive, process; and the solutions will vary widely across different social and legal settings. Nonetheless, basic research will be a universal precursor to success, and it is here that collaborative international effort can have the greatest positive impact on mitigating future violent extremism.

Appendix H

Psychology of Transnational Terrorism and Extreme Political Conflict

Scott Atran, Research Professor
University of Michigan/Oxford University

This contribution provides highlights of a report discussed at National Academy of Sciences–Russian Academy of Sciences workshops.

SUMMARY CONCLUSION

1. The goal of transnational terrorism is to degrade, and then replace, the political order by first driving people into clashing sociopolitical camps, with no room for innocents.
2. Regardless of its likelihood to create physical harm, terrorism has outsized psychological, social, and political effects on public health and policy.
3. Extreme forms of terrorism—and other highly committed revolutionary and radical forms of violence—are enacted by devoted actors defending or advancing nonnegotiable sacred values rather than by rational actors who primarily weigh material costs and benefits to achieve goals.
4. Field studies of frontline combatants, together with behavioral and brain studies of radical populations, indicate that people are more willing to fight and die for sacred values than for nonsacred values.
5. In some extreme circumstances, commitment to sacred values can outweigh commitment to any group, including family and close comrades.

6. Preventing extreme violence, and resolving seemingly intractable conflict may require addressing an adversary's sacred values rather than ignoring or denigrating them, while also directly engaging (particularly with youth) in the social networks that give life to those values.

7. Social media today do more to encourage than to discourage radicalization and extreme polarization, owing to the particular psychological and structural affordances of internet platforms and channels for networking.

8. The increasing sociopolitical polarization over values in open societies creates an existential challenge: By impeding deliberative decision-making and blocking democratic consensus, these divisions deepen existing susceptibilities and widen opportunities for further degradation from terrorism.

FUTURE ISSUES

1. Insofar as social marginalization of individuals and political polarization of groups both seem to promote sacralization of nonsacred values and willingness for costly sacrifice, what underlying cognitive and neuropsychological processes might they share?

2. We know little of the cognitive processes by which mundane values become sacralized or desacralized (e.g., white supremacy was a sacred value for mainstream Americans and Europeans at the beginning of the 20th century, but it is now most prevalent in society's fringes) or how these processes might be slowed or accelerated to relieve conflict.

3. How to preserve social bonds of family, community, and transgenerational continuity, especially in times of conflict and adversity in societies that favor individual decision-making and cost-benefit analysis, is a psychological issue critical to liberal democracies.

4. How might use of the internet and social media help rather than hinder people's ability to tolerate contrary and diverse beliefs and opinions, achieve consensus, and negotiate solutions to conflicts?

5. In the psychology of persuasion and how ideas become contagious in an era of so-called fake news, what factors disfavor recourse to reason, evidence, and truth while favoring recourse to psycho-social biases (e.g., entrenched belief and confirmation biases, in-group and authority biases, negativity focus, bandwagon effect, etc.) in

promoting extreme violence? And how can these factors be parried to convince people to abandon political violence?

For additional views: Atran, S. 2020. "Psychology of Transnational Terrorism and Extreme Political Effect," prepared for the 2021 *Annual Review of Psychology*. Ann Arbor: University of Michigan.

Appendix I

Recent Trends and Future Concerns in Worldwide Terrorism

Professor Gary LaFree
University of Maryland

Researchers have long noted that terrorism rises and falls in waves (Rapoport, 2002; LaFree, Dugan, and Miller, 2015). According to the Global Terrorism Database (GTD) collected by the National Consortium for the Study of Terrorism and Responses to Terrorism, or START, at the University of Maryland, the world has been gripped by a wave of terrorist attacks that began shortly after the 9/11 attacks. From 2002 through 2014, worldwide terrorist attacks increased nearly 12-fold (from 1,333 to 16,903), and terrorist fatalities increased by more than 8 times (from 4,805 to 44,490). Especially hard hit were Iraq and Afghanistan in the Middle East, India and Pakistan in South Asia, and Nigeria in Sub-Saharan Africa. The most active terrorist organizations in driving this worldwide boom were the Taliban, Al-Shabaab, the Islamic State, the Communist Party of India (Maoist), and Boko Haram.

But since 2014, the picture has changed dramatically. According to the GTD, 2019 was the fifth consecutive year of declining global terrorist attacks (Miller, 2020). Total attacks worldwide decreased 50 percent between 2014 and 2019, and the total number of deaths decreased 54 percent. This is the single largest 5-year decline in attacks and fatalities since the GTD began data collection in 1970—a half century ago.

To be clear, terrorist attacks and fatalities are not declining everywhere and every year. In 2019, attacks and fatalities increased in Yemen, Colombia, and Burkina Faso; in 2018, attacks and fatalities increased in Afghanistan and Nigeria; and in 2017, attacks and fatalities increased in India, the Philippines, and Nepal. Also, while worldwide attacks have declined, a large number of countries are still being targeted: more than 100 different countries in recent years.

It is also important to emphasize that not all reasons for declines in terrorist attacks are positive. For example, an argument can be made that in several years when terrorist attacks declined in Afghanistan, they did so in part because the Taliban had been so successful in taking back control of the country (Felbab-Brown, 2017; Nordland, 2018). A similar outcome but with the regime rather than the terrorist perpetrators gaining control of the situation no doubt explains declining terrorist attacks and fatalities in Syria (Cook, 2018).

While we have observed major declines in terrorist attacks and fatalities from 2014 to 2019, both attacks and fatalities remain at historically high levels. The number of attacks in 2019 is about the same as in 2012 and attacks are still more than 40 percent higher in 2019 than they were during 1992—the peak year for an earlier wave.

At present, the GTD is only available through the end of 2019. However, in late December of that year, a previously unidentified coronavirus, now called COVID-19, emerged from Wuhan, China, quickly spread throughout China, then expanded globally, eventually affecting all countries of the world. To the best of my knowledge, at the time of this writing there are no published empirical studies dealing with the impact of COVID-19 on terrorist attacks and fatalities. However, there are several reasons to believe that the COVID-19 pandemic could increase the number and deadliness of terrorist attacks. While societies are preoccupied with responding to the pandemic, it could open up opportunities for terrorist perpetrators to plan and carry out attacks. Moreover, epidemics might increase economic and political stress, sharpen individual frustration, and thereby encourage radicalization and extremist violence. On the other hand, the pandemic could hamper the ability of would-be terrorists to perpetrate terrorist activity as much as it has hampered a host of noncriminal activities.

As we move into 2021, a number of terrorism-related developments appear on the horizon. While the Taliban engages in peace talks with the United States, terrorist attacks and fatalities associated with the group continue to mount. In 2019, Afghanistan accounted for 41 percent of worldwide terrorist fatalities (including assailants) and 21 percent of all terrorist attacks (Miller, 2020). While Islamic State violence continues to decline in Iraq, the group's international reach continues to grow. By 2019, the Islamic State and its affiliates had staged terrorist attacks in a total of 57 countries (up from 21 in 2014). Boko Haram continues to be extremely active in Nigeria, and in

2019, it also increased its activity in Cameroon, Chad, and Niger. In 2019, there was a sharp increase in the number of attacks motivated by various strands of far-right extremism in Australasia, North America, and Western Europe. It remains unclear to what extent these attacks are being fueled by anger and frustration over government efforts to combat COVID-19.

One thing is certain: the number of terrorist attacks in a particular region or the world as a whole will eventually reach an apogee and then decline. What goes up must eventually come down. It seems logical to conclude that the chaos and disorder that follow in the wake of terrorist attacks provide strong incentives for societies to adopt strategies for countering them. Few individuals or communities prefer living endlessly in chaos and violence. As the deadly impact of COVID-19 eventually subsides, we can only hope that we have reached that tipping point. At the same time, we must humbly admit that prediction is the most precarious task of the social sciences.

Sources

Cook, S. A. 2018. "The Syrian War Is Over, and America Lost: Bashar al-Assad Won. It's worth thinking about why the United States didn't." *Foreign Policy*, July 23. https://foreignpolicy.com/2018/07/23/the-syrian-war-is-over-and-america-lost/.

Felbab-Brown, V. 2017. "Afghanistan's Terrorism Resurgence: Al-Qaida, ISIS, and Beyond." https://www.brookings.edu/testimonies/afghanistans-terrorism-resurgence-al-qaida-isis-and-beyond/.

LaFree, G., L. Dugan, and E. Miller. 2015. *Putting Terrorism in Context: Lessons from the Global Terrorism Database.* London: Routledge.

Miller, E. 2020. *Global Terrorism in 2019.* College Park: University of Maryland, START. https://www.start.umd.edu/pubs/START_GTD_GlobalTerrorismOverview2019_July2020.pdf.

Nordland, R. 2018. "The Death Toll for Afghan Forces Is Secret. Here's Why." *New York Times*, September 21, 2018. https://www.nytimes.com/2018/09/21/world/asia/afghanistan-security-casualties- taliban.html?rref=collection%2Ftimestopic%2F Taliban&action=click&contentCollection=timest opics&region=stream& module=stream_unit&version=latest&contentPlacement=1&pgtype=collection.

Rapoport, D. C. 2002. "The Four Waves of Rebel Terror and September 11," in *The New Global Terrorism: Characteristics, Causes, Controls*, C. W. Kegley Jr., ed. Upper Saddle River, NJ: Prentice Hall.

Ward, A. 2014. "Do Terrorist Groups Really Die? A Warning." *The Rand Blog*, posted December 2, 2014. https://www.rand.org/blog/2018/04/do-terrorist-groups-really-die-a-warning.html.

Appendix J

Labor Migration and Radicalism

Academician Vitaly Naumkin
Institute of Oriental Studies

This report exemplifies how National Academy of Sciences–Russian Academy of Sciences discussions have contributed to broader analyses of important issues.

The workshops held involving Russian, American, and French counterparts provided opportunities to have constructive exchanges of opinions as well as to engage in the discussion of some of the most crucial issues facing the current global agenda. We used the key takeaways of the meetings and discussions in carrying out our academic research and experimental studies. One of the most important aspects raised was the radicalization of labor migrants, who arrived in Russia from the Central Asia states.

Labor migration from the Central Asia states to Russia allows those states to solve their problems related to unemployment and exacerbating demographic situations, whereas Russia, at the expense of labor migrants, fills vacancies in its labor market, especially those that are not attractive to local residents.

The overwhelming majority of labor migrants coming from the Central Asia states have arrived in Russia to obtain an income and solve financial problems experienced by their families, primarily the men. The vast majority of labor migrants note that one can always find a job in Russia that might not be highly paid necessarily, but guarantees stable earnings. If you are Russian-speaking and you have a professional qualification, then there is a chance you can obtain a well-paid job. Some labor migrants often try to take advantage of their stay in Russia to learn new skills and trades. There are some who find it much more exciting to work in Russia rather than in their own villages in the middle of nowhere. The greater part of migrants come to Russia for seasonal work. Some plan to stay in Russia for a longer period, even permanently. The highest desire to secure Russian citizenship is harbored by the Kyrgyz and the Tajiks, and to a lesser degree by the Uzbeks.

Most of the migrants who have succeeded in being granted Russian citizenship have been integrated into new communities quite well. Their children receive a good education and enjoy an opportunity to get ahead in life using the social elevators. However, there are a minority who prefer to lead their own lives and continue to mingle predominantly with like-minded individuals representing their ethnic background. This model of behavior can lead to a recurrent migration challenge facing the European Union member states, where children of migrants in their third or fourth generation, including migrants of well-off families, end up sharing radical views.

The labor migrants from the Central Asia states are capable of hard work and acting at their own initiative. They are not arrogant or egoistic. These qualities are valued by their employers. According to the labor migrants' estimates, there is less corruption in Russia and more freedom of speech than in their own native countries, they do not have to give bribes to obtain a good job, and there is no religious persecution. The most important issue is not to break the law.

The respondents from some labor migrants—residents of Tajikistan and ethnic Tajiks who have been granted Russian citizenship—have proved to be more open in responding to surveys than the labor migrants from Uzbekistan.

Ethnic Kyrgyz, in contrast to ethnic Uzbeks and Tajiks, have exhibited a more tolerant and accommodating attitude toward religious matters. Among the migrants, especially those who have a higher educational background, some individuals are not concerned with religious matters at all. Moreover, some consider themselves atheists. The greater part of the polled Kyrgyz believe that neither religious leaders nor the Mosque play a significant role in radicalization. At the same time, they believe that the religious factor does have an impact on a part of the Uzbek community residing in the south of the Kyrgyz Republic. The Kyrgyz Uzbeks have appeared to be aliens in their own country. However, they have not been accepted as insiders by the ethnic Uzbeks from the Republic of Uzbekistan.

Such is the tragedy of the second largest ethnicity in the Kyrgyz Republic. The residents of Tajikistan first come by themselves and then bring their families along. The residents of Uzbekistan stay in Russia without their families more often than not. As a consequence, there are a lot of split or broken families among the Uzbeks and Tajiks alike. This is another problem that needs to be solved.

The educational level of the Central Asia migrants has been decreasing over the years, and in 2020, in connection with the pandemic, the number of migrants in Russia has been lower than before due to the difficulties associated with travel across the borders. The number of migrants who have a good knowledge of Russian that would allow them to adapt to the new environment without any problem has been also decreasing. Most of the labor migrants learn about the new developments from the electronic media outlets and the web sources. The social media feature the communities whose memberships includes kinfolk and fellow countrymen.

The processes of radicalization underway in the modern world that sometimes lead to full-scale armed conflicts known to evolve into civil wars in some countries in the Middle East have affected labor migrants from the Central Asia states, too. Meanwhile, the radicalization of labor migrants from Central Asia has not expanded to a massive scale on Russian territory. There is no hard-and-fast answer to the question: Where exactly does the radicalization of labor migrants from Central Asia take place? Judging by the outcome of conducted polls, the prerequisites or fundamentals for the radicalization are laid down in the native countries of labor migrants. The most vulnerable group is made up of young people below 20 years of age, who are not burdened with families, who have a low level of general and religious education, who do not wish to earn their living by fair means, but who strive to get everything straight away with no consideration of moral norms or principles. For the most part, these individuals become the target of recruiting strategies by the Jihadist emissaries.

The basic reasons underlying the radicalization phenomenon are poverty, social inequality, and no possibility of finding a job that would allow proper support of a family in the native country. The important factors include the state's refusal to perform its social responsibilities, the decline of general education, the emergence of sociocultural barriers, and the destructive activities of extremist prophets. This has been most conspicuous in the Kyrgyz Republic, primarily in the south of the country, and also in Tajikistan.

For many migrants, religious parties and groups, such as Hizb ut-Tahrir al-Islami in Kyrgyzstan, became useful platforms for the migrants' active engagement with local Muslims in seeking to disrupt traditional and tolerant forms of Islam. The respondents to polls noted on multiple occasions that the recruiting process had been initiated by certain "Caucasians," while the daily organizational work was carried out by fellow countrymen in most cases.

As our discussions with colleagues suggested, the mechanisms and methods of recruiting, the human and material resources involved, the financial support, and the connections with the security services and organized crime groups that helped to make recruiting of volunteers into the ranks of terrorist formations a profitable business have all been important. They should be among the topics of independent and comprehensive research.

The poor command of the Russian language by labor migrants is an important reason why they cannot sustain their rights when they encounter law enforcement officers, formalize adequately the authorization documents and labor arrangements with their employers, and interact with the Russian community. Their children have difficulty in communicating with Russian children in their age group and in attending preschool and general education establishments.

Moreover, migrants are often unaware of the fundamental principles underlying the Russian migration legislation and the procedure and regulations for the issuance of authorization documents. They may feel compelled to ask assistance from all sorts of black market wheeler-dealers, who deceive the migrants and profiteer off their problems. As a result, the deceived migrants either join the ranks of illegal migrants or, if they are caught with forged documents, they are deported from Russia on a condition that they are further banned from entering Russia for a certain period.

A positive role for the migration from Uzbekistan has been played by the Agreement between the Government of Uzbekistan and the Government of the Russian Federation, signed in April 2017, "On the Streamlined Selection and Drawing of the Citizens of the Republic of Uzbekistan to Carry Out Temporary Labor Activities on the Territory of the Russian Federation." A Russian Migration Center for the Streamlined Selection of Citizens to Work in Russia has been opened in the city of Samarkand, and a Permanent Representation Office of the Russian Foreign Ministry has been established in the city of Tashkent to manage the selection process of candidates seeking to work in Russia. Some success has been achieved in the Central Asia states in socioeconomic development, notwithstanding the handicaps related to the COVID-19 pandemic. This success has played a part in preventing radicalization of labor migrants leaving for Russia.

The closely coordinated efforts undertaken by the government agencies of Russia, Uzbekistan, Kyrgyzia, and Tajikistan; by civil society structures; and by nongovernmental organizations have been very instrumental in the destruction of the financial basis for recruiting that had been turned into a lucrative business by the organized crime groups. There have been harsh and inevitable punishment of the recruiters and their henchmen.

Appendix K

References

DOCUMENTS THAT RESULTED FROM INTER-ACADEMY COOPERATION

Cross-Cutting Activities and Issues

Schweitzer, G. E. 2004. *Scientists, Engineers, and Track-Two Diplomacy: A Half-Century of U.S.-Russian Interacademy Cooperation*. Washington, DC: The National Academies Press, ch. 4.

Ethnic Conflicts within Russia, the Greater Middle East, and North Africa

Abdulaeba, Kh. R., and A. D. Yandarov (eds.). 2002. *Annotated Bibliography of the Chechen Conflict*. Moscow: Institute of Ethnology and Anthropology (in Russian only).

Gakaev, D. D., and V. A. Tishkov. 2003. *Peace in Chechnya through Education* (report of a workshop in Sochi). Moscow: Institute of Ethnology and Anthropology (in Russian only).

Hellenberg, T., and K. Robbins (eds.). 2006. *Proceedings of a Workshop: Root and Routes of Democracy and Extremism*. Helsinki: Aleksentari Institute, University of Helsinki.

NRC (National Research Council). 2003. *Conflict and Reconstruction in Multiethnic Societies: Proceedings of a Russian-American Workshop*. Washington, DC: The National Academies Press.

NRC. 2004. *The Path to Peace in Chechnya: Stages, Tasks, and Prospects* (student essay competition in Grozny). Washington, DC: The National Academies Press.

NRC. 2010–2011. Informal notes of three workshops, two in Moscow and one in Washington, D.C. "Turmoil in the Middle East: Primakov-Pickering Dialogs."

NRC. 2017. Informal notes of a workshop in Moscow. "Opportunities for Inter-Academy Collaboration on Violent Extremism."

NRC. 2017. *Improving Understanding of the Roots and Trajectories of Violent Extremism: Proceedings of a Workshop–in Brief.* Washington, DC: The National Academies Press.

NRC. 2019. *Developments in Violent Extremism in the Middle East and Beyond: Proceedings of a Workshop–in Brief.* Washington, DC: The National Academies Press.

Tishkov, V. A. 2004. *Ethnology and Politics* (2nd ed.). Moscow: Institute of Ethnology and Anthropology (in Russian only).

Tishkov, V. A. (ed.) 2005. *Multiethnic Societies during Transformation: The Experience of Dagestan* (material from a conference in Moscow). Moscow: Russian Academy of Sciences (in Russian only).

Acceptable Limits on Biological Terrorism

Netesov, S. 2013. *Security Aspects of Biological Research in Central Asia* (report of a training program). Novosibirsk: Novosibirsk State University (in English).

NRC (National Research Council). 1997. *Controlling Dangerous Pathogens: A Blueprint for U.S.-Russian Cooperation: A Report to the Cooperative Threat Reduction Program of the U.S. Department of Defense.* Washington, DC: The National Academies Press.

NRC. 2006. *Biological Science and Biotechnology in Russia: Controlling Diseases and Enhancing Security.* Washington, DC: The National Academies Press.

NRC. 2007. *The Biological Threat Reduction Program of the Department of Defense: From Foreign Assistance to Sustainable Partnerships.* Washington, DC: The National Academies Press.

NRC. 2009. *Countering Biological Threats: Challenges for the Department of Defense's Nonproliferation Program Beyond the former Soviet Union.* Washington, DC: The National Academies Press.

NRC. 2013. *The Unique U.S.-Russian Relationship in Biological Science and Biotechnology: Recent Experience and Future Directions.* Washington, DC: The National Academies Press.

Radiological Challenges: Security, Sources, Waste Sites, and Disposal

NRC (National Research Council). 1999. *Protecting Nuclear Weapons Materials in Russia.* Washington, DC: The National Academies Press.

NRC. 2003. *End Points for Spent Nuclear Fuel and High-Level Radioactive Waste in Russia and the United States.* Washington, DC: The National Academies Press.

NRC. 2005. *An International Spent Nuclear Fuel Storage Facility: Exploring a Russian Site as a Prototype: Proceedings of an International Workshop,* G. E. Schweitzer and A. C. Sharber, eds. Washington, DC: The National Academies Press.

NRC. 2006. *Strengthening Long-Term Nuclear Security: Protecting Weapon-Usable Material in Russia.* Washington, DC: The National Academies Press (in English and Russian).

RAS (Russian Academy of Sciences). 2007. *Cleaning Up Sites Contaminated with Radioactive Material,* A. Plate, ed. Moscow: Russian Academy of Sciences.

NRC. 2007. *U.S.-Russian Collaboration in Combating Radiological Terrorism.* Washington, DC: The National Academies Press.

NRC. 2008. *Setting the Stage for International Spent Nuclear Fuel Storage Facilities: International Workshop Proceedings,* G. E. Schweitzer and K. Robbins, eds. Washington, DC: The National Academies Press (out of print).

NRC. 2009. *Cleaning Up Sites Contaminated with Radioactive Materials: International Workshop Proceedings*, G. E. Schweitzer, F. L. Parker, and K. Robbins, eds. Washington, DC: The National Academies Press.

NRC. 2019. *The Convergence of Violent Extremism and Radiological Security: Proceedings of a Workshop—in Brief.* Washington, DC: The National Academies Press.

NRC. 2020. *Scientific Aspects of Violent Extremism, Terrorism, and Radiological Security: Proceedings of a Workshop—in Brief.* Washington, DC: The National Academies Press.

Security of Transportation, Industrial, Construction, Communications, and Other Urban Challenges

NRC (National Research Council). 2002. *High-Impact Terrorism: Proceedings of a Russian-American Workshop.* Washington, DC: The National Academies Press (in English and Russian).

NRC. 2004. *Terrorism: Reducing Vulnerabilities and Improving Responses: U.S.-Russian Workshop Proceedings.* Washington, DC: The National Academies Press (in English and Russian).

NRC. 2006. *Countering Urban Terrorism in Russia and the United States: Proceedings of a Workshop.* Washington, DC: The National Academies Press (in English and Russian).

NRC. 2009. *Countering Terrorism: Biological Agents, Transportation Networks, and Energy Systems: Summary of a U.S.-Russian Workshop.* Washington, DC: The National Academies Press.

NRC. 2009. *Russian Views on Countering Terrorism during Eight Years of Dialogue: Extracts from Proceedings of Four U.S.-Russian Workshops.* Washington, DC: The National Academies Press.

OTHER DOCUMENTS THAT PROVIDED BACKGROUND FOR THIS REPORT

Cronin, A. K. 2017. *Power to the People. How Open Technological Innovation Is Arming Tomorrow's Terrorists.* Oxford: Oxford University Press.

Gambetta, D., and S. Hertog. 2016. *Engineers of Jihad.* Princeton, NJ: Princeton University Press.

Hecker, S. S., ed. 2016. *Doomed to Cooperate.* Los Alamos, NM: Bathtub Row Press.

Hoffman, B. 2017. *Inside Terrorism.* New York: Columbia University Press, ch. 1.

Khabriev, R. U. 1997. *Russian Joint Stock Company Biopreparat.* Moscow: Biopreparat.

Leitenberg, M., R. A. Zalinkas, and J. H. Kuhn. 2012. *The Soviet Biological Weapons Program.* Cambridge, MA: Harvard University Press.

NAS (National Academy of Sciences). *Meeting of Official Delegations of the Russian Academy of Sciences and the U.S. National Academies in Moscow on the 50th Anniversary of Scientific Cooperation,* June 2009.

NRC (National Research Council). 2002. *Making the Nation Safer. The Role of Science and Technology in Countering Terrorism.* Washington, DC: The National Academies Press.

NRC. 2019. *The Role of Social Sciences Research in National Security. Highlights from Three National Academies Reports.*

NRC. 2019. *A Decadal Survey of the Social and Behavioral Studies: A Research Agenda for Advancing Intelligence Analysis.* Washington, DC: The National Academies Press.

Office of the Director of National Intelligence. 2021. "Global Terrorism," in *Annual Threat Assessment of the U.S. Intelligence Community.* Washington, DC, April 9.

Orlov, K. V., and F. F. Svetnik. 2006. *Analysis of the Risks and Problems of Security.* Security of Russia Series, vol. 4. St. Petersburg, Russia: Znanie (in Russian only).

Russian Ministry of Education. 2002. *Assessment Report: Education in the Chechen Republic: Conditions, Problems, and Perspectives of Restoration and Development.* Moscow/Grozny (in Russian and English).

Schweitzer, G. E. 1997. *Experiments in Cooperation: Assessing U.S.-Russian Programs in Science and Technology.* New York: Twentieth Century Fund Press.

Shoigy, S. K. 2005. *Emergency Service of Russia 1990–2005.* Moscow: Ministry for Civilian Protection, Emergencies, and Elimination of the Results of Dangerous Situations (in Russian only).

White House. 2018. *National Strategy for Counterterrorism of the United States of America.* Washington, DC: National Counterterrorism Center.